'*Vertical Growth* lays out a clea[r] <barcode> grow as human beings. It is a m[...] making the world a better place, and who understands that self-awareness is now even more critical in our fragile workplaces.'

Paul Hutton, Vice President, APAC, Hilton

'This is essential reading for any leader who wants to get the very best out of themselves, their teams and their organisation. The challenge to deeply understand what drives each of us as leaders, and to honestly challenge our own behaviours and the impact on the team and the organisation, is both unique and inspiring.'

Michael Wright, Executive Chairman & CEO, Thiess

'This book clearly shows how self-awareness enables leaders to grow and make an even greater impact for and with their people. A wonderful read, inspiring, practical and insightful.'

Jerh Collins, Chief Culture Officer, Novartis

'Michael Bunting's approach makes a profound difference. I have personally seen his work transform people for the better. This new book delivers an elegant, compelling process for real growth in leaders.'

Peter Horgan, CEO, Omnicom MediaGroup, ANZ

'One of the hardest challenges we face as leaders is getting people to change. What this book reveals is that the easiest and best way to get others to change is to change ourselves. This book is for any leader ready for that life-changing commitment.'

Elaine Lim, Asean Talent Development Leader, EY

'Michael Bunting's work is life-changing. This book is his best work yet. It codifies a clear process for genuine transformation in leaders and cultures and takes us far beyond where we thought we could go.'

Aimee Buchanan, CEO, GroupM Australia & New Zealand

'Every leader should read this book. It will help you understand why people struggle to change and what you can do to enable yourself and others to reach their full potential. An enjoyable, educative read—I highly recommend it.'

Radoslava (Radi) Anguelova,
Head of Corporate Human Resources, Swarovski

'This book brilliantly reveals the secret inner world that really drives leaders. It helps us to choose wisdom over fear, values over self-centredness and awareness over numbness to become the best leader we can be.'

Jason Smith, SVP & President, International,
Allergan Aesthetics, an AbbVie company

'This book helps us understand why we so rarely find leaders who truly walk their talk and why those who do are exceptional. It reveals the inner world that drives our actions and decisions, and lays out a clear map to eliminate the gap between what we think, what we say and what we do. This is the book to read if you want to really understand the why, what and how of self-awareness and team psychological safety.'

Commodore Eric Young, CSC, RAN,
Director General Navy People

Vertical Growth

HOW **SELF-AWARENESS** TRANSFORMS **LEADERS** AND **ORGANISATIONS**

MICHAEL BUNTING
WITH **CARL LEMIEUX**

WILEY

First published in 2023 by John Wiley & Sons Australia, Ltd

Level 1, 155 Cremorne St, Richmond Vic 3121

Typeset in Abril Tilting 11 pt/15pt

© Worksmart Australia Pty Ltd, 2023

The moral rights of the authors have been asserted

ISBN: 978-0-730-39551-5

A catalogue record for this book is available from the National Library of Australia

Cover design by Wiley
Cover image by © Anita Ponne/Shutterstock

Disclaimer
The material in this publication is of the nature of general comment only, and does not represent professional advice. It is not intended to provide specific guidance for particular circumstances and it should not be relied on as the basis for any decision to take action or not take action on any matter which it covers. Readers should obtain professional advice where appropriate, before making any such decision. To the maximum extent permitted by law, the authors and publisher disclaim all responsibility and liability to any person, arising directly or indirectly from any person taking or not taking action based on the information in this publication.

Printed in Singapore

M WEP173311 211222

Contents

Free bonus resources

To make the most of this book, make sure to sign up to our companion web app at mymatrix.themindfulleader.com

- Easy-to-use tool to map your vertical growth journey
- Complete real-life case studies mapped for you
- Additional resources to support your understanding

Author's note

Throughout this book we feature case studies from 26 top global leaders at Novartis, EY, Amryt Pharma, Sanofi, Lonza, Takeda Pharmaceuticals and Ubisoft. (Note that while we work with a wide range of industries, in the process of writing this book we were focused heavily on pharmaceutical companies.) The majority of these leaders attended a rigorous leadership development program with me over a period of 12 to 18 months, and I have a personal relationship with all of them. A large percentage of them are or were from Novartis, simply because much of our breakthrough thinking evolved as a result of working with their top 300 global leaders in an 18-month leadership development program. While this book was being edited, Novartis underwent a major corporate restructure, which means that some of the Novartis leaders featured in the book have been promoted or moved and some are now making the world a better place in other important organisations.

We can never express enough gratitude to the leaders who shared their real and vulnerable stories for this book. You are our 'why', you make this world a better place. Thank you.

Michael Bunting

INTRODUCTION
The vertical growth imperative

'The snake that cannot shed its skin must perish.'
Friedrich Nietzsche

Sheila Frame, President of the Americas for the pharmaceutical company Amryt Pharma, shared with me her past experience of work days spent putting out one fire after another. There were times when she struggled with proactively setting an agenda and creating a plan for her team, and when her team members didn't really know what was expected of them, she would step in and solve problems for them.

She became aware of this self-defeating pattern and what was creating it only when she went through a vertical growth training program. As she explained to me, 'I started to realise that my resistance to planning, goal setting and proactivity came from my wanting to keep my options open, because I like to be in the action. I'm a master at managing a crisis. It's an adrenaline rush for me and I love it. So why would I be more proactive when it would cut off my opportunity to be in the centre of all the action?'

Until Sheila experienced this moment of self-awareness, goal setting or proactive planning skills were of little value to her. She would simply revert to her default behaviour pattern. She was driven by her unconscious need for the short-term gratification of managing crises, which took precedence over her aspiration to create a more strategic focus in her team.

Sheila first needed to see this pattern to realise how she was contributing to the team dysfunction. This is what self-awareness and vertical growth are all about, and why they are far more important for long-term leadership success than leadership theories, tools and techniques. Instead of reacting to challenges and opportunities based on our programmed algorithms, we develop enough awareness to recognise our algorithms in action and question their value.

Self-aware people who, like Sheila, embrace a vertical growth mindset see themselves as a continual work in progress and become progressively less afraid to look at themselves honestly. Through the process of developing self-awareness, they begin to realise that their dysfunctional patterns of behaviour have nothing to do with their self-worth.

This realisation is a pivotal growth moment. They understand that all human beings, even the best of us, have conditioned patterns of behaviour, and these patterns can be recognised, questioned and changed, and are therefore logically not who we fundamentally are. With this understanding, their growth accelerates. They take things less personally and are less interested in defending and protecting their image and more interested in becoming more aware and adaptive in a complex world. As leadership expert Edwin Friedman observed, 'Leaders who are willing to make a lifetime commitment to their own continual self-regulated growth can make any leadership theory or technique look brilliant.'

Horizontal skills and knowledge versus vertical growth

In our work, we differentiate between horizontal development and vertical growth. Horizontal development is about acquiring knowledge and developing new skills to bring about a new competency.

While improving horizontal competencies may require repeated practice, it typically requires no growth in self-awareness or self-regulation. Simple examples might be learning planning skills or mastering MS Word or Excel.

In a leadership development context, it can be easy to confuse leadership development principles and training with vertical growth. For example, the leadership techniques and practices needed to 'enable others to act' or to apply 'agile methodology' are typically taught as a set of horizontal skills, learnable by any leader, regardless of his or her level of self-awareness and maturity. The mistake we often make is that when these skills are applied poorly or inappropriately, we assume the techniques and skills we were taught were inadequate. This is rarely the case. It's a vertical growth challenge.

Vertical growth involves both *downward seeing* and *upward growth*. We see downward (vertically) into our unconscious patterns of thought and behaviour and learn to deal with them with awareness, patience and compassion. The more we do this, the more we increase our ability to grow upward in the direction of our values, aspirations and ideals. Through vertical growth, we are able to train our mind to engage less in the reactive and programmed algorithms of our mind and body, and more in a deliberate and flexible set of behaviours based on our aspirations and values.

In short, as illustrated in figure I.1 (overleaf), with vertical growth we explore downward in ourselves to resolve our deep-seated assumptions, fears and patterns in order to grow upward into our best selves. It's an 'inside-out' job rather than an 'outside-in' job. This, combined with basic behavioural science (prompts, rituals and the like) and the necessary horizontal skills, delivers on the promise of amazing leadership and healthy cultures. We can briefly summarise the two forms of development as follows:

- **Horizontal development** means developing the skills and gaining the knowledge I need to work in the organisation to get my job done efficiently, effectively and safely.

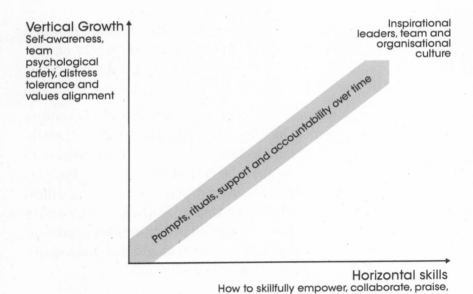

Figure I.1: vertical versus horizontal development

- **Vertical development** means developing the ability to change how I perceive and value my inner and outer world (mindset), then building the self-regulating awareness to support the development of new behaviours in a sustainable way aligned with my core values.

This book focuses on vertical growth and presents a detailed process for going about it, on both a personal and organisational level.

In leadership development, personal behaviour change or culture change, horizontal development is just not enough. Leaders may learn the specific skills of strategic planning, conflict management, productivity improvement and empowerment on the assumption that understanding the what and how is enough for the skills to be applied and embedded. Organisations may publish new values statements, explain them really clearly and educate people on their importance on the assumption that it will result in culture change. But it will not.

Horizontal development is extremely important, even in the complex field of leadership development and culture change, but alone it's a false promise. It is not enough, because horizontal skills and knowledge compete with fears, limiting beliefs and other mental models that keep us locked in habitual patterns and reactive loops. Seeing and changing these loops is the function of vertical development.

In leadership terms, this is when 'walking the talk' becomes far more consistent. A term we like to use in our work is the *self-examined mind*. This is the stage of development in which a person consciously authors his or her values and daily behaviour, instead of being trapped in the unconscious reactivity of what Harvard development experts Robert Kegan and Lisa Lahey call *image management*.

Image management refers to the time and energy we waste in organisations on blame, denial, deflection, defence, gossiping, politics, saving face, masking our weaknesses and other fear-based strategies to make ourselves feel safe or look good. Kegan and Lahey maintain that image management is a second job for most people in typical organisations. One research study we performed involving more than 5000 people from various global organisations indicated that image management may suck up about 40 per cent of people's time and energy on average. This is a staggering waste of time and energy, costing billions of dollars.

More critically, image management creates values breaches, wherein people fail to speak up or admit mistakes, judge or blame others, and avoid addressing inefficiencies—all to ensure their image is protected. This arrests growth, damages leadership credibility, shuts down innovation and impacts mental health, while keeping relationships superficial.

Margaret Dean, Head of People and Organisation at Novartis Oncology, shared with me her view of vertical growth as about recognising and dissolving her self-defeating patterns. She explained, 'One of the key insights in my process was to start seeing the stories and patterns I have developed as a way of protecting myself. I've had to reflect and be deliberate about letting go of them in order to create the life I want. It's much easier just to ignore these patterns and keep living them. But when I'm willing to peel back the layers of the onion and ask myself if this is really what I want, I can see what's not serving me and holding me back.

'So growth for me is about letting go of old beliefs and patterns and replacing them with awareness and curiosity to enable the development of more thoughtful, mindful ways of behaving. This requires us to always push ourselves out of our comfort zone where we can learn something new.'

With vertical growth, we are no longer looking outward but rather are turning inward. We're bringing a level of precise awareness to our inner thoughts, emotions, sensations and behavioural patterns. We're questioning why we behave in certain ways, why we are emotionally triggered by certain things.

Vertical growth requires a willingness to face tremendously difficult truths about our thoughts and behaviours while cultivating an attitude of kindness and patience towards ourselves. The amazing payoff is an increased capacity to choose our behaviours with insight, wisdom and compassion.

As Paul Spittle, Chief Commercial Officer of General Medicines at the biopharmaceutical firm Sanofi, told me, 'Vertical growth is having a better understanding of your thoughts, emotions and behaviours. And related to that, allowing yourself to accept some things that you wish weren't true about your behaviour and thinking, then asking, "What do I do about that? How do I use that?" We have an incredible capacity to deny the worst things about our behaviour, but if we can't face these things, we can't work on them or develop further.'

Paul's colleague Kevin Callanan, a Senior Vice President of Sanofi, added, 'For me, vertical growth is being able to stop and look at situations and my emotions. The more I look, the more I can separate my ego or wants and desires from what is best for the team or organisation as a whole. I have more clarity and I make better, more informed decisions. I also have more empathy towards others and inner peace.

'And that's not an easy thing to do, especially for someone like me who has a thirst for action and a thirst to respond. So there's always that inner conflict between my immediate desire to move quickly and get things done, and my desire to slow down and be more conscious and deliberate.'

Brian Gladsden, Head of Worldwide Commercial and Portfolio Strategy at Novartis Oncology, put it even more simply, 'To me, vertical growth comes from being clear on my personal values, but more importantly, the real growth comes from *feeding* those values. Am I nourishing what's most important to me?'

To use an analogy, horizontal development is like having a computer operating system such as Microsoft Windows and adding apps like MS Word, Whatsapp and other useful programs to facilitate our work. But vertical growth is about changing the entire operating system to generate more power and manage greater complexity. That then enables a much smarter use of the apps and programs.

Vertical growth within organisations

The head of culture for a multinational division once called us for strategic advice. I asked her what she had implemented so far. She had been busy with endless events and webinars on a huge range of relevant and interesting subjects. Her people were practically drowning in cool events and awesome guest speakers.

'How effective has it been so far?' I asked.

She was silent for a moment, before admitting with embarrassment that the culture and leadership behaviour was as bad as ever.

She was implementing what we call an 'information spray-and-pray' approach to development, throwing masses of information at people, hoping at least some of it would stick and actually change behaviour. But all the information and skill building in the world are not enough to deliver long-term, significant sustainable cultural change. We need to go deeper.

A common mistake organisations make that contributes to this wasted investment is believing that cultivating self-awareness and personal growth are a matter of developing new skills or gaining new knowledge. Unfortunately, this simplistic approach entirely misses the point.

Focusing on horizontal skills and training without vertical growth is like planting a flower in poorly fertilised soil. Unable to take root or gain the necessary nourishment to grow, it cannot flourish and will inevitably just wither away. An organisation can spend millions of dollars training its leaders in horizontal skills and knowledge, but it's a poor investment unless it's preceded and supported by vertical growth (and the use of behavioural science). Without a foundation of vertical growth, our ability to apply horizontal skills and knowledge wisely is limited, although, ironically, we typically remain in denial of these limitations. To change our behaviour we must first see it and explore it objectively in order to best understand where it comes from as well as cultivate the ability to manage it in real time.

One client we worked with was interested in developing accountability and a growth mindset in their organisation. They introduced the concept of 'victim versus players' borrowed from another leadership development provider. They wanted 'players' in their teams—people who did not make excuses or play victim, but were proactive and had a can-do attitude. Unfortunately, it quickly became apparent that applying this concept in their culture was backfiring. When someone challenged an idea or way of working, or challenged poor behaviour in an attempt to hold people accountable, they were accused of being a victim.

Many well-intentioned people within the organisation were embodying a player mentality, but the lack of self-awareness and vertical growth in many of the leaders resulted in a distortion of the intention behind the principles. A 'player' became someone who agreed to any request, worked unreasonable hours and accepted poor behaviour. This is why it is so dangerous to ignore vertical growth. All too often, wonderful horizontal knowledge and skills end up getting twisted into the very opposite of their intent.

With vertical growth training, we transcend the unconscious emotional and reactive brain to connect with our higher-order brain functions that allow us to self-regulate as well as make more informed and creative decisions. Vertical growth enables us to more readily bypass the conditioned reactions that have kept us safe over the years but now hold us back from our full potential and deepest happiness.

Furthermore, personal vertical growth enables leaders to empower and develop their people. Susanne Schaffert, President of Novartis Oncology, shared with me why vertical growth is important to her, 'When it comes to dealing with a crisis, what leaders are asked for is not specific skillsets. It goes much deeper than that. What we are asked to do is inspire people toward achieving common goals. We are asked to energise and comfort people and give them confidence. The biggest impact we can have as leaders is not what we personally do with our skills, but rather what we inspire our people to do through our character. And how can we become inspirational leaders if we are not grounded, balanced and mindful? It's impossible.'

Vertical growth cuts through image management

'So, Pat, how did it go with your boss, Robin?' I asked.

'Not great,' Pat replied.

'What happened?'

'Well, after we completed that anonymous survey on Robin's leadership, we were invited to a meeting to discuss the results. When we got into the meeting, the very first thing Robin said was, "Team, thanks for the feedback. There's good stuff in there, but I just want to say that you have all rated me poorly on empowerment, and I totally disagree with your ratings. I know I'm great at empowering you."

'The entire team and I just sat there and nodded in agreement. We were wrong, Robin was right. Robin left the meeting smiling, we left feeling disengaged once again. I remember promising myself I'd never be honest again. What's the point? But, you know, pretty much every boss I've had has been the same.'

Sadly, defensiveness, denial and even blame occur every day in organisations, families and relationships. Instead of taking a self-aware, growth-mindset approach to life's challenges, like Robin we often defend our self-image to protect ourselves from emotional discomfort. We don't do this because we are dishonest or because we don't want to grow. Rather, we have been hijacked by our primitive brain and the old coping mechanisms that were designed to help us manage difficult feelings like overwhelm, fear, hurt and insecurity.

To add to this, our research indicates that less than 10 per cent of us have been educated on how to regulate our emotions, handle challenging feedback and cultivate self-awareness. Is it any wonder that we so often choose protection over growth, image management over vulnerability and numbness over facing difficult feelings?

This phenomenon negatively impacts mental wellbeing, careers, families, teams, organisations, even nations. It ensures we keep repeating behaviour patterns that don't serve us or others well. This is the price tag of a lack of self-awareness and the associated absence of a vertical growth mindset.

Given that up to 40 per cent of an organisation's time and energy may be wasted on image management, it's no wonder that engage-ment levels in organisations are so low. In the second half of 2021, for example, Gallup reported that employee engagement rates in the United States had dropped to a dismal 34 per cent. The ratio of engaged to actively disengaged workers in the US is 2.1 to 1, down from 2.6 to 1 in 2020.[1]

As humans we are hardwired for self-protection and survival, which includes the need to please and be accepted by our tribe. Managing one's image is a modern-day survival mechanism. We can spend a lifetime in this mode without consciously noticing it, including enjoying a brilliant career and accomplished life, as seen through the lens of society. So why do we need self-awareness and vertical growth?

Behind the gloss of image management, we can actually suffer tremendously. The vast majority of accomplished leaders secretly experience 'imposter syndrome'. If we dig a little deeper, they will admit they need validation to deal with deep insecurities. (McKinsey & Company coined the term the 'insecure overachiever' to describe this global phenomenon.) As a result, they struggle with being truly values-based. Andre Viljoen, CEO of Fiji Airways, calls this phenomenon 'the plastic hero'. No amount of external success will ever make Pinocchio (our self-image) a real boy or girl. The fancy titles, and the deference and privilege that come with them, are not who we are. Secretly, we know this, and we dread the inevitable loss of this image.

The greatest privilege of our careers has been earning the trust of exceptionally talented and successful people who have had the courage to admit that image is not satisfying, that one never reaches a golden moment when image management results in deep self-acceptance and true inner peace. We have worked with wonderful people who have grown beyond the need for protection and image approval and sought out a life of inner exploration, personal growth and internal congruence to find a profound sense of joy, meaning and resilience.

This is the purpose of developing self-awareness and embracing vertical growth. We are blessed with an amazing mind–body system that has an astonishing capacity for lifelong learning, the development of noble, inspiring qualities, and the realisation of profound inner congruence and wellbeing. Those who can unleash this capacity can make a profound impact on culture, performance and wellbeing in organisations.

This is why we are particularly passionate about focusing on leaders. The research shows that nothing impacts people's work experience and performance more than the behaviour of those in leadership roles. Having self-aware leaders who consciously self-lead within an organisation is how we create values-based, high-trust innovative organisations that build people up and increase psychological safety, wellbeing and performance in today's increasingly complex and uncertain world.

Why self-awareness is critical

A self-aware person can view their thoughts, emotions, conditioned patterns and reactions objectively. Through the development of self-awareness, we become present, compassionate, honest, curious, committed and transformational. The greater our self-awareness, the greater our capacity to align our behaviour with our noblest intentions and values.

Conversely, the less self-aware we are, the more we are subject to our unconscious thoughts, beliefs and assumptions as well as the conditioned patterns and behaviours that move us away from our best self with all of its potential.

Nurturing and protecting an image involves a fundamental confusion in the mind. As a result of childhood conditioning, what people think of us comes to determine our self-worth, and slowly but surely we disconnect from our core and become lost in patterns that soothe that loss. This is why the journey into authenticity and self-awareness is both challenging and extraordinarily rewarding. It's our journey back home to ourselves. We come to see that image management is exhausting and sustains a perpetual sense of imposter syndrome.

Leaders who embrace the self-awareness journey become a beacon of growth and psychological safety for those around them. Instead of denying their mistakes, they are honest with themselves and others. They are interested, even excited, by seeing behaviours in themselves that are not working and they are courageous enough to admit it. Instead of justifying, ignoring and denying actions that hold them back from deeper insight and wiser choices, they want to understand where, how and why they're falling short on their values and aspirations. And by doing so they give others the safety and permission to do the same.

Becoming deliberately developmental

Cultivating our capacity for growth is a lifelong journey, not a short course. Leadership expert John C. Maxwell recounts, 'The first year I engaged in intentional personal growth, I discovered that it was going to be a lifetime process. During that year, the question in my mind changed from "How long will this take?" to "How far can I go?"'

But *how* do we intentionally grow, particularly as adults, when our beliefs and behaviours have become ingrained in us? What does it even mean to grow? And how does it work in groups and organisations?

Intentional vertical growth requires us to be *deliberately developmental*, meaning we apply conscious and deliberate practices that help us grow as human beings. When leaders become deliberately developmental, it becomes possible to do this growth work as an entire organisation. Kegan and Lahey call this a Deliberately Developmental Organisation (DDO).

In this book, you will first learn how to develop a self-aware, psychologically safe growth mindset in yourself. Part I focuses on understanding how our brain works to hijack our best efforts and how to train our brain to work for us rather than against us. We introduce the Mindful Leader Matrix, our formal tool for helping leaders and organisations become deliberately and consistently values-aligned, growth-based and psychologically safe.

Part II reviews the central role of developmental mindfulness in the self-awareness process. Here we will dig deep into vertical growth to gain a greater context for applying the Mindful Leader Matrix.

Finally, in Part III, we will examine how you can apply the process within your team and organisation. You will learn how to hold yourself and others accountable in healthy ways that promote positive growth and psychological safety, rather than fostering distrust and resentment. You will learn a detailed process for building a Deliberately Developmental Organisation (DDO) which will lead to improved productivity and effectiveness. The 40 per cent of your people's time that is currently wasted on image management can be redirected toward learning, innovation and growth.

In short, you will learn the core practices that support lifelong vertical growth, enabling you to lead consistently in a way that inspires and makes your world, and that of others, a better place. Far from being an expression of naïve idealism, it is becoming increasingly clear that people expect these results from businesses and other institutions. Our client EY expresses this beautifully in their core purpose: 'Building a better working world'.

Cultivating inner psychological safety

As Sanofi's Paul Spittle suggested, cultivating self-awareness inevitably elicits a deeper level of honesty with ourselves. We begin to see the full range of our thoughts, assumptions, feelings and behaviours, much of which we were previously in denial about or numb to. When we do, our most common response is to judge and reprimand ourselves for our 'bad' feelings, thoughts, assumptions and behaviours. As a result, we very quickly lose two of the most important vertical growth tools: curiosity and compassion.

There can be no learning or new insight without curiosity. As the great depth psychologist A. H. Almaas said in a lecture I attended,

'Without the emotional safety compassion provides us, we very quickly lose interest in uncovering difficult truths we need to deal with. It's too painful to look at, so instead we shut down and go back to familiar coping mechanisms such as blaming others, denying and numbing.'

This is why we must encourage self-compassion and curiosity around why this behaviour is present. Self-compassion gives us a space of inner psychological safety, which enables our natural curiosity and intelligence to come to the fore. This compassion and curiosity also enables us to boldly try new behaviours, to stumble, to take chances and experiment, to learn and grow without that harsh inner critic beating us up over the inevitable mistakes we make.

Self-compassion expert Kristin Neff, co-founder of the Center for Mindful Self-Compassion and author of *Self-Compassion: The Proven Power of Being Kind to Yourself*, states the obvious: 'Self-compassion is a healthy way of dealing with the pain of life. By definition, there's no downside to it.'

Margaret Dean, at Novartis Oncology, shared with me how easy it is for her to shame herself when she sees herself falling into the same old controlling, image management patterns with her team members. Mindfulness has taught her to interrupt this pattern in the moment. She said, 'I always compound my behaviour by beating myself up, which only makes things worse. For me it feels like a shameful feeling, like I need to take a shower. My brain asks over and over, *Why did you just do that? Why didn't I see that in the moment?* But I'm learning to tell myself, *That's part of being human. It's okay. Everyone screws up once in a while.* And I can hold it more lightly and more easily look at my behaviour with curiosity and interest instead of judgement and shame.'

Psychological safety is also vital for growth, innovation and trust in a team setting. We will discuss in great detail how to create an environment of psychological safety in Part III. In our experience, leaders who learn to cultivate self-compassion for themselves then become more caring and compassionate with their teams.

UC-Berkeley Professor of Psychology Serena Chen writes in a 2018 *HBR* article, '... self-compassion encourages a growth mindset is also relevant here... Research shows that when leaders adopt a growth mindset...they're more likely to pay attention to changes in subordinates' performance and to give useful feedback... Subordinates, in turn, can discern when their leaders have growth mindsets, which makes them more motivated...'

Research on vertical growth and mindful leadership

The process and practices we detail for you in this book have been developed over many years. They are the synthesis of a staggering amount of research and a wide variety of leadership cognitive and behavioural sciences as well as mindfulness disciplines.

We started teaching elements of this transformational leadership work in 2001. In 2008 we integrated Jim Kouzes and Barry Posner's 'five practices of exemplary leadership' because we wanted more research around our own leadership work. Kouzes and Posner's work is incredibly well researched. Over the past 30 years they have accumulated data that now includes 5000 individual case studies, five million survey respondents, data from 70 countries and 700 research studies by others. Based on rigorous testing of reliability and validity, it's the most independently researched leadership model on Earth.

In 2015, I co-authored a book with Kouzes and Posner, drawing on their five leadership practices and their application in the Australia and New Zealand context. In 2016, I published two more books, *The Mindful Leader* and *A Practical Guide to Mindful Meditation*.

The Mindful Leader owes its foundations to the extensive leadership research by Kouzes and Posner and introduces two additional leadership skills, self-awareness and accountability, alongside vertical growth elements.

When *The Mindful Leader* was published, we created a 360° assessment to measure and research the mindful leadership practices themselves, and we added correlation outcomes, such as engagement and mental health. We wanted to measure the impact of leaders applying mindful leadership on key personal and organisational outcomes. Our first study involved 328 self-assessments and 3380 overall responses in some of the biggest companies in the world.

What we found was that the percentage of engagement accounted for by mindful leadership is an astonishing 40.16 per cent. This essentially means that for every 10 per cent a leader improves in these mindful leadership practices, their direct reports are 4 per cent more engaged. Nothing impacts organisational performance more than leadership—particularly mindful leadership.

We also found that a third of people's mental health can be explained by their bosses' behaviour, as measured in these mindful leadership practices. So leaders who improve their mindful leadership increase not only the engagement but also the mental wellbeing of their team members.

To support these findings, we have developed a training program and online course, which we have called *The Mindful Leader: Vertical Growth*. It's available on our Awakened Mind mobile app and is used by leaders all over the world. Our initial research showed that those who used the program improved their team's psychological safety, trust, growth mindset and values-based behaviours by 31 per cent over a 16-week period.

I share these resources with you to demonstrate that the principles of conscious development and mindful leadership are real, tangible and measurable. Furthermore, they are *learnable* by anyone willing to accept the challenge of self-awareness.

PART I

Developing a vertical growth mindset

1
The Mindful Leader Matrix

'Have no fear of perfection; you'll never reach it.'
Marie Curie

In 2019, three years after publishing *The Mindful Leader*, we asked ourselves this question: What are the absolute core vertical growth competencies all leaders and teams must know in order to continuously grow and be exceptional? In other words, regardless of the horizontal skills and knowledge they need—for example, skills to support accountability, empowering others and conflict management—what vertical growth will still be needed to ensure success in the application of these horizontal skills?

Once we had a clear answer to that question, our next practical question was how to simply and elegantly represent the process of vertical growth on a single page. After much work, we developed what we now call the Mindful Leader Matrix.

The Mindful Leader Matrix (figure 1.1, overleaf) drew on a variety of key sources, including Steven Hayes' Acceptance Commitment Therapy (or Training) (ACT), Robert Kegan's work on immunity to change, and the advanced transformational leadership and self-awareness practices we have researched and developed through our work with leaders and organisations around the world.

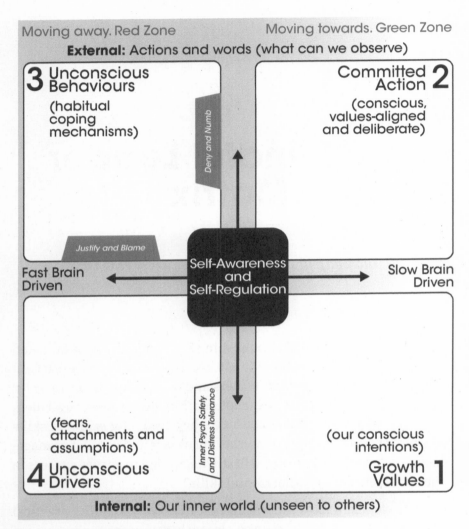

Figure 1.1: the Mindful Leader Matrix

Our new and original formulation of the matrix also allows for culture change and organisational development work. This represents the culmination of 20 years of study, research and practice in the areas of leadership, team and culture development.

How to use the matrix

The horizontal axis shows us moving either towards or away from our growth values and conscious intentions. The zone on the right represents our values, aspirations, purpose and healthy desired behaviours. The zone on the left represents unconscious and conditioned responses, quick-fix solutions, short-term rewards and pain avoidance.

The bottom area of the horizontal axis represents our internal world of feelings and mental models. Inside this area we also find the unconscious values we have adopted from our parents, teachers and society since birth. Our mental models are the framework with which we interpret and perceive the world. They are deeply rooted in our unconscious. While they operate in the present, they are constructed from the past—often the very distant past, as our brain is most plastic in our early years and defines our ego structure for decades to come. These mental models have typically been reinforced at critical stages of our lives; they determine our psychological flexibility and shape our actions.

The less self-awareness we have of our mental models, the more psychological rigidity we will have. This means our thoughts and behaviour can be a little like a repeated recording. We play out similar responses to variable realities. For example, a leader might micromanage others inappropriately as a conditioned response to fear of losing control. In his childhood he may have experienced trauma while having no power or control, then developed a fixed mental model that insisted on always maintaining high levels of control. This may have been useful in extreme circumstances and may have helped him cope with the early trauma, but it leads to a rigid, repeated set of behaviours that become problematic and disconnected from reality in later life.

This is what we mean by rigidity. Our past conditioning is rigid and fixed. The human brain evolved over millions of years to find quick fixes in our early years and to wire that in for future coping needs.

The more self-awareness we develop, the greater our psychological flexibility. This opens our mind to increased possibilities. We move away from self-preservation and towards expansion, as we mindfully see our mental models more clearly and can make choices to overcome them. For example, it might be quite appropriate to micromanage in an extreme emergency, and be completely inappropriate to do as a daily leadership practice. The self-aware leader can do both, depending on what is actually needed. In other words, she has developed psychological flexibility.

The top area of the horizontal axis represents our external world: our words, actions and behaviours. Behaviours can be reactive or impulsive when they emerge from what is called our 'fast brain', also referred to as our mammalian or limbic brain. Or they can be deliberate and values-based when we are able to self-regulate our emotions with our 'slow brain', emerging from our more advanced prefrontal cortex and other cortical areas, and have clarity on what is important to us. We'll explain the brain science in more detail later. The more we are committed to the right side of the matrix, the easier it is to have agency over the left side, and the greater our capacity to make conscious choices in life. The less self-awareness we have, the less we will cultivate our growth mindset and explore our full potential.

The vertical axis divides our world into the conscious, values-based, self-regulated choices on the right and the quick-fix, numbing, conditioned, fear-based responses on the left.

The Mindful Leader Matrix can be summarised as follows:

- **Quadrant 1** in the lower right represents our growth values, which pull us in the direction of our conscious intentions. Rather than assumed values that have been handed down to us from parents and society, this is where we consciously choose values that will enable us to vertically grow to become more conscious, balanced human beings, leaders and organisations that make the world a better place.

- **Quadrant 2** in the upper right represents the conscious, committed actions we take to move towards quadrant 1 and change our unconscious behaviour. From a leadership perspective, this is what we commit to and practise to ensure we actually walk the talk we formulated in quadrant 1.

- **Quadrant 3** in the upper left represents the behaviour that flows from habit and our unconscious fears, attachments and assumptions. This is what we are doing when not moving towards the right side of the matrix. These are the habitual coping mechanisms that provide us with short-term relief from our discomfort or quick rewards, while usually damaging our relationships, diminishing our influence, wasting our time and energy and preventing us from achieving our intent and commitments in quadrants 1 and 2.

- The 'Deny and Numb' and 'Justify and Blame' tabs in quadrant 3 are important to understand, as they keep us locked into quadrant 3 behaviours and prevent us from exploring quadrant 4's unconscious drivers. The numbness and denial element—what we call the 'first line of defence' against our shadow—literally enables us to not fully notice or take accountability for our unconscious 'moving-away' behaviours. The justification and blame element is what we call the 'second line of defence' against the shadow. This occurs when we break through the first line of defence (numbness and denial) and acknowledge quadrant 3 behaviours, but very quickly justify them or blame others. In doing so, we fail to take the next step into understanding our deeper fears, attachments and assumptions in quadrant 4, while continuing to engage in our quadrant 3 behaviours.

- **Quadrant 4** in the lower left represents our unconscious fears, attachments and assumptions (our conditioning) that drive our moving away behaviours and ensure resistance to our commitment in quadrant 2. This is the realm of our internal mental and emotional baggage that holds us back from achieving our full potential. We see and take accountability for our quadrant 3 behaviours. This is what Carl Jung called 'shadow work', as it describes the exploration of our unconscious behaviour and its drivers, our ego or the unknown and darker side of our personality that we wish to move away from. This part of ourselves was often conditioned in our earlier, formative years or through traumas or difficult experiences.

- The tab labelled 'Inner Psychological Safety and Distress Tolerance' in quadrant 4 represents the two core skills we need to explore our shadow. Without them, our inner work is too confronting and we fall prey to the first and second lines of defence. Among other factors, inner psychological safety refers to self-compassion and curiosity. Distress tolerance refers to our ability to accept and handle difficult emotions without running from them through defence or numbing mechanisms. The more distress tolerance we cultivate, the more we are able to stay curious and growth-minded in the face of emotional discomfort and pain.

- Self-awareness and self-regulation are placed in the middle of the matrix, as without self-awareness and the ability to consciously regulate our behaviour, we cannot deliberately live a values-based life, nor can we learn to see, accept and compassionately take accountability for the shadow that moves us away from our best intentions.

Fast brain, slow brain

As you can see, the left side of the matrix is 'fast-brain driven', while the right side is 'slow-brain driven'.

Research by neuroscientists Joseph LeDoux and Matthew Lieberman sheds light on why we can sometimes get stuck in our habitual behaviours and engage in pain avoidance and quick-fix solutions, rather than pushing through discomfort to move towards our values and a more meaningful life. According to LeDoux, our brain has two pathways through which the amygdala's fear responses can be triggered: a fast 'low road' from the thalamus to the amygdala, and a slower 'high road' that passes from the thalamus to the prefrontal cortex and only then to the amygdala (see figure 1.2, overleaf). He explains that these two systems don't always reach the same conclusions.

Lieberman refers to these two pathways as the 'X-System', which is reactive (a fast pathway), and the 'C-System', which is reflective (a slow pathway), meaning it gives us time to reflect and make more conscious choices (see figure 1.2, overleaf).

This fast brain is a product of evolution and is part of our mammalian brain. It has served us well over the years, enabling us to escape from predators and avoid social rejection, both of which could make the difference between life and death. The brain has essentially not changed much since those hunter-gatherer days and is still wired the same way. According to the National Science Foundation, the average person has between 12000 and 60000 thoughts per day. Of those, 95 per cent are repetitive thoughts and 80 per cent are negative, designed to keep us safe from potential predators and risks.[2]

The fast brain thus engages the parts of the brain that act spontaneously and impulsively (our emotional centres). The slow brain, on the other hand, is linked to our more recent brain development that differentiates us from other mammals. These more evolved neural structures, such as the prefrontal cortex and its executive functions, engage parts of the brain that enable us to act with intention and awareness before our fast-brain reflex response takes over. This system also helps regulate the emotional fight, flight or freeze reactivity of the fast brain.

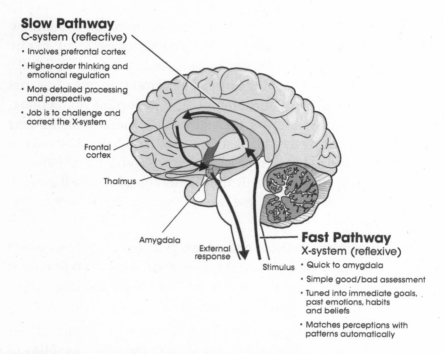

Slow Pathway
C-system (reflective)
• Involves prefrontal cortex
• Higher-order thinking and emotional regulation
• More detailed processing and perspective
• Job is to challenge and correct the X-system

Frontal cortex

Thalmus

Amygdala

External response

Stimulus

Fast Pathway
X-system (reflexive)
• Quick to amygdala
• Simple good/bad assessment
• Tuned into immediate goals, past emotions, habits and beliefs
• Matches perceptions with patterns automatically

Figure 1.2: what keeps us away from our values and aspirations
Source: Brain image: © Blamb/Shutterstock

When the reactive fast brain is triggered by something we perceive as a threat, the slower brain is suppressed as hormones surge through our bloodstream and neurotransmitters flood our brain. As a result, we respond impulsively and lose our ability for self-awareness and self-regulation. The reactive parts of our brain take over and we become defensive. We don't see things objectively. We don't listen well to others because our brain is consumed with defending against a threat. In the modern world, we often perceive interactions as threats, when the only thing they really threaten is our self-image.

The reactive fast brain is focused on past emotional memories, short-term goals, habits and beliefs. When operating from the fast brain, our responses are emotional, conditioned and habitual. The brain matches perceptions with patterns automatically, which shuts down curiosity, learning and growth. If we don't cultivate self-awareness, it's the unconscious mind or fast brain that's really in charge.

The slow brain, on the other hand, gives us the ability to become the observer, broaden our perspective, think more logically and creatively, see things with more clarity and wisdom, and ultimately choose new behaviours. The job of the slow brain is to challenge and correct the fast brain.

To master growth requires that we bring mindfulness to fast-brain reactions, which sabotage our long-term goals, and operate more from the slow brain or prefrontal cortex in order to move towards our values and goals. To shift from our fast to our slow brain, we need self-awareness and the ability to self-regulate, as we will discuss in greater detail in Part II. We can also shift from the fast brain to the slow brain by having clear intentions and deliberately choosing our values and responses, rather than being held hostage by quick habitual responses.

When operating from the reactive fast brain, external events trigger our unconscious beliefs, which then trigger unconscious, conditioned actions and behaviour. Overcoming these instinctive reactions requires two things: (1) replacing unconscious fears, beliefs and assumptions with presence, awareness and consciously chosen values (internal work); and (2) aligning our thoughts and behaviours with our values (actions that support our internal aspirations).

It's pointless to choose our desired path forward and underlying values without a daily commitment to deliberately cultivating those values in action. As a leader, for example, you will note that your team members don't experience your *aspirations*; they experience your *behaviour*.

To begin our vertical growth journey, our invitation is to move towards our values in the right zone of the matrix, while being aware of the left zone, changing our unconscious behaviour through committed action. As obvious as this may appear, this concept is actually counterintuitive as it requires us to move away from our comfort zone and develop a high level of self-awareness as we shift from being seduced by the dopamine rush and reward system that is activated when we avoid short-term discomfort or seek out pleasures and rewards.

The Mindful Leader Matrix is all about moving from fast-brain reactivity to slow-brain proactivity. It's about defining what you really want to further develop in your life and/or your leadership, then cultivating that through clear intent and committed action. In the following chapters, we walk you through each one of these elements and help you create your own Mindful Leader Matrix.

You can create your own personal, team and/or organisational matrices by logging in to mymatrix.themindfulleader.com. Figure 1.3 illustrates what the online template looks like.

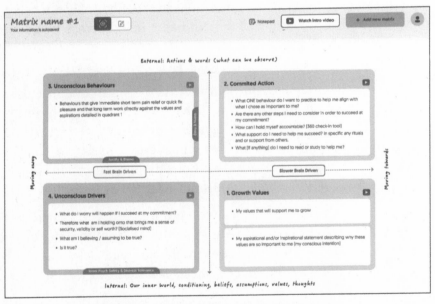

Figure 1.3: Mindful Leader Matrix example

You'll find useful additional free tips and resources on the website. Your Mindful Leader Matrix will be a powerful resource in helping you organise your development journey, one that you will revisit and use again and again.

2
Why leaders struggle with walking their talk

'There is no favourable wind for someone who does not know where they are going.'

Lucius Annaeus Seneca

When we introduce our clients to the Mindful Leader Matrix, we always start at the bottom right. In a leadership context, it begins with the simple question, 'What is the talk you are trying to walk as a leader?' In other words, what is most important to you to role model both as a human being and as a leader? What are your values, your code, the principles you want to lead by?

All leaders need to answer this most obvious question because it has such a deep connection to trust and credibility. In fact, research by James Kouzes and Barry Posner, the co-authors of my first book, concludes that leaders who can communicate their talk clearly are 66 per cent more trusted than those who can't. Fascinatingly, however, we have found it extremely rare for leaders to be able to answer this question.

We've always wondered why some people are clear about following virtuous leadership principles such as honesty, generosity, kindness and curiosity even under pressure, and some people aren't, and why some people take them seriously and some don't. Why do some people think they are acting from these virtues when they are not, and why are some people more honest with themselves than others. The obvious answer, of course, is that although they may be highly skilled and competent, incongruent leaders lack vertical growth.

Stages of human development

We've introduced the Mindful Leader Matrix as a formal process for leaders to identify their values (talk), then to choose behaviours that put those values into action (walk). But before we get deeper into how to use the matrix, we first need to stress why it's so difficult to use in the first place. A deeper understanding of how our brain works and how we develop as adults gives us both context and motivation for navigating the matrix. So before we take you through the more specific questions, reflections and techniques on working through your own development matrix, let's first look at adult development and how it informs your self-awareness and personal development journey.

Adult development psychologist Robert Kegan developed what he termed the *subject–object theory*, which provides a model of how the human mind develops vertically over time. 'Subject' represents patterns of thinking, feeling and behaving we are identified with but are not consciously aware of, and therefore cannot reflect on, view objectively or change. 'Object' refers to patterns of thinking, feeling and behaving we are able to consciously reflect on, look at, take control of and be responsible for.

What we are 'subject to' is that which governs how we make sense of the world. It is an element that determines our experience but that itself cannot be questioned or examined. It is either taken as true or not even considered at all. Robert Kegan shares an anecdote of a very young child, say three years old, who is subject to his immediate sense perceptions. If the child were to look down on a street from the top of a tall building, he might think, *Wow, those cars are tiny!* A few years later, he might find himself at the same vantage point and think, *Wow, those cars* look *tiny!*

In this example, the child's visual perception shifts, so something they were previously *subject to* (that is, it couldn't be questioned or challenged) they can now hold *as object*, allowing them to examine and question whether things really are as they appear. This small shift actually reflects very significant developmental growth, through which sensory perceptions no longer govern and circumscribe one's understandings of reality. Rather, one can recognise that the world conforms to certain physical laws even when our senses might fail to accurately apprehend these processes.

The process of vertical growth is about 'making object' the patterns of thinking, feeling and behaving that we were previously 'subject' to, so we can view them from a more objective perspective and be less driven or controlled by them. Some of this occurs naturally, especially in the earlier stages of development, and some occurs through deliberate practices, especially in the more advanced stages.

Babies start at stage zero of development, completely subject to their reflexes. They cry, urinate or kick with no conscious awareness or control over these natural reflexes. The first stage of development, the 'impulsive mind', starts around age two, when the child can begin to hold her reflexes as object. She is subject to her impulses—like grabbing from another person's plate or hitting someone who took her toy. But physiological reflexes/movements can be consciously chosen.

Before too long, the impulsive mind naturally develops into the next vertical stage, the self-centred mind. Now the child has some agency over her impulses. Impulses she was subject to, like urinating, have now become object to her. She notices the impulse and has some choice as to when and where to urinate. This is the process of subject–object theory. The self-centred mind is completely subject to what it wants in the moment, with limited awareness or consideration of long-term goals or other people around them.

To best overcome this short-term gratification mechanism, we need to understand that humans develop in stages, and each stage comes with its own level of awareness, control over our behaviour and values that drive our behaviour. The lower our stage of development, the more our unconscious impulses, thoughts, assumptions, fears and desires rule us. The higher our stage of development, the more our unconscious impulses, thoughts, assumptions, fears and desires become object or conscious to us and the more choice and agency we have over them.

So what enables us to see the bigger picture and assert control over our impulses, thoughts, assumptions, fears and desires? Adapting Kegan's work, figure 2.1 helps us to explain the process.

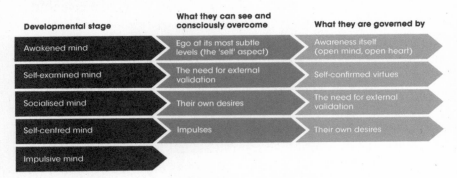

Figure 2.1: adult development simplified

The self-centred mind

The first development milestone we reach is the *self-centred mind*, or what Robert Kegan refers to as the self-sovereign mind. The self-centred mind is subject to our desires, as we don't yet have the awareness or discipline to put them aside. At this stage, we have little to no empathy for others. The value system revolves around our 'getting what we want'. Kegan quips that in this stage a child will sell his mother for 50 cents to buy candy. This stage is typically associated with young children, but for some (Kegan estimates as much as 15 per cent of the adult population), it can actually persist throughout their lives. *Arther*

The socialised mind

As most people mature, they move naturally into a third stage called the *socialised mind*. In this stage, we begin to exercise control over our own desires in order to fit into a family, group or organisation. We feel empathy for and connect with others. This is a considerable growth achievement for our species.

Using a marshmallow example, if you give a child at the self-centred mind stage two marshmallows, he will most likely eat them himself. If he does share, it will only be if he sees that it is to his future advantage. But if he has developed a socialised mind, he may be more inclined to share the marshmallows with a friend, because a friend's concerns and interests have become internalised. The friend's satisfaction can be experienced as one's own satisfaction. He curbs his self-centredness in order to belong to a group, which requires that he cooperate and collaborate with others.

However, this shift is not necessarily driven by a sense of care for others. Rather, it is usually about seeking approval and a sense of belonging. In a socialised mind, our self-worth depends more on what other people think about us, and less on our own beliefs about ourselves. It comes from who we are in the eyes of others and our place in a social group. Our unconscious values revolve *Cre* around feeling socially safe and being liked and/or admired. Rather than following values for their own sake, we are unconsciously obsessed with the question, 'What do other people value and how can I be that?' We haven't yet realised that following values is a more rewarding process than being ruled by our need for group acceptance or admiration.

Margaret Dean, at Novartis, shared with me what this looks like for her. 'I often fall into patterns of trying to stay in control or avoid looking stupid. This often leads me to do what will make me look good in the moment, rather than living according to what's really important to me. For example, there have been moments when I wanted to speak truth to power, but I wasn't brave enough to do it. I just told them what they wanted to hear.'

(I want to point out here that the fact that Margaret can speak of her fears with this level of self-awareness indicates that her centre of gravity has advanced beyond the socialised mind.)

Our need for approval typically takes two forms. The first is the need to impress. This too can come in many forms, including showing off a fancy car or home, winning awards, having a fancy job title or needing to sound intelligent. It's craving to be in the limelight and to be appreciated. One common form of this is wanting to be the expert. We may boast of degrees, books published or university tenure, for example, to seek approval.

Another form of approval-seeking is trying to be a 'nice' person. We don't confront others; we may even avoid the limelight, because we want to be liked.

My friend Grant and I enjoy playing tennis together. I have a hangover tendency to want to be a star and impress people. Grant, on the other hand, is the type of person who really wants others to like him. So whenever we play tennis I always try to beat him to ensure I am seen as a 'winner', while he always tries to let me win to be liked!

James Skinner, the Oceania Executive Development Coach at EY, admitted to me that his values were once chosen from his socialised mind. 'In the past when I did values exercises, I would always pick things like fairness, kindness and compassion. I didn't recognise that I was strongly influenced by my need to fit in, to belong and to be accepted.

As a result, my delivery of those values could be used to conveniently create belonging for me, rather than genuinely helping others.

'I've had to ask myself if my values are authentically true to me, or whether they were pushed onto me by my parents or society. And it goes all the way back to when I was in school. I was a member of every group, but not at the core. I was selected for leadership positions because of my ability to get along with everyone.

'As I've aged and matured, I've realised that I have sacrificed a lot for this belonging and acceptance. I often haven't expressed my true feelings, I've allowed people to take advantage of me, and I haven't stood up for myself. I also haven't delivered clear and direct feedback when I should have at times.

'I've had an unconscious assumption that I could simply win everyone over to me through kindness, fairness and compassion. It's been devastating for me to learn that some people haven't fully trusted me because they see that I just try to get along with everyone.'

It's very difficult for the socialised mind to challenge the system or to be truly innovative within an existing organisational system. Its goal of fitting in or being the best and brightest at what the organisation currently values is directly at odds with new ways of doing things. It's good at being good at what the system rewards, and good at avoiding behaviours that might risk social exclusion or rejection.

Most of the general population is at this stage of development, because most people don't make it past the socialised mind stage, and those who do are likely to regularly revert to this stage under stress or perceived threat.

The self-examining mind

The stage that comes after socialised mind is referred to by Kegan as the 'self-authoring mind'. A smaller percentage of the general population is likely to achieve this stage of development. The shift from socialised mind to self-authoring mind begins when we ask the question, *What is important to me and what do I stand for aside from what anyone else thinks?* We connect with our own heart and determine our own values and moral compass.

The self-authoring mind sees the need for external validation in the socialised mind. Once that need can be seen as *object*, we can consciously choose our own values. We are no longer subject to our need to be liked or admired or to belong. As one of our clients put it, 'We can move from a motivation to *look* good, to a motivation to *do* good, even if we look bad doing it.' Our needs and values are communicated to those around us who matter most without the fear of being judged or excluded.

We can stop being swayed by peer pressure and choose our own path in life, rather than simply fitting in. In the more advanced stages of the self-authoring mind—what we call the 'self-examining mind'—we are willing to sacrifice our need to be liked or to belong for the sake of our personal values. In other words, we begin to really walk our talk.

After much discussion with industry experts, including Robert Kegan's associates, it became clear to us that developmental mindfulness practices and philosophies add a deeper, more deliberate element to 'self-authoring' than is typically meant or described by the term. In this more self-aware stage, values are not only clear and self-confirmed, but are also utilised as a means to consciously interrupt fear-based, habitual reactions. Over time, fear is reduced in the mind and body, while awareness, inner stability and ease increase. In mindfulness terms, the inner work required to consciously and deliberately live a virtues-based life supports deep inner stability, which opens the door to much more refined levels of self-awareness (and vertical growth).

The self-examining mind is moving closer to the awakened mind described below and correlates closely with adult development expert Susanne Cook-Greuter's 'eighth stage of development', which is described as 'focused on becoming the most one can be; guided by big picture principles; thriving on human complexity and variety, as viewed from a coherent, complex, and separate core sense of self; alive and aware that what one sees depends on level of development; creative; inclusive and pragmatic leadership'.[3]

The key distinction from Kegan's model, and why we call it something different, is the emphasis we place on releasing fear and fear-based reactivity through conscious training and transforming. We are not concerned with academic perfection, but rather with the *process* required to truly lead from wholesome values that make the world a better place, and to personally create a profound sense of inner congruence and wellbeing. After combined decades of working with tens of thousands of leaders, and using the world's most validated leadership model as a base for leadership development, we are confident that this is the right descriptor and process for leaders who want to truly walk their talk; make the world a more conscious, caring, ethical and fairer place; and consciously and deliberately grow while becoming happier and wiser.

The self-examining mind has answers to the following questions:

- *How do I know this thinking is useful?* (mental models)— understanding and leveraging one's own beliefs and values through directly examining experience, rather than depending on external influences for shaping one's thoughts and values.

- *What do I stand for?* (intrapersonal)—understanding and committing to one's values, being concerned with personal integrity, aligning actions with values.

- *How do I want to construct relationships with others?* (interpersonal)—understanding one's role in society, being aware of feelings and relationships instead of being subject to them.

- *What is life asking me to be?* (transpersonal)—bypassing the ego structure, which allows us to see what emerges from a place where no barriers get in the way.

- *How do I honour my internal commitments?*—understanding that every decision we make is an opportunity to move us closer to what we want and to expressing our authentic selves. This includes regularly checking in with ourselves and having the courage to ask others to call us out when we move away from our authentic self.

There's a reason why Socrates famously said, 'The unexamined life is not worth living.' In the socialised mind we're trapped by fears, denials and delusions. Our sense of self-worth and inner stability depend on the external world and other people's validation of us. In the self-examining mind, we begin to fully comprehend the psychological suffering in the numbness, delusion and helplessness of socialised mind. As our previously fractured mind settles into a new congruent home of ease, awareness and aliveness, we begin to understand that integrity is not a set of ethical rules, but rather a profound experience of wholeness.

Kevin Callanan, at Sanofi, shared a story with me that illustrates this. Before entering the corporate world, Kevin was a self-employed lawyer. One company he represented was a product manufacturer. One of their products, which generated millions in revenue a year, was subject to reported concerns of misuse by the customer, creating health issues. So Kevin approached his client and advised them to move away from the product to maintain integrity in the market.

A representative of one of the companies they manufactured this product for approached Kevin and offered him $250 000 to stop his resistance to the product, in a way that would not be illegal. Kevin recalled, 'I remember in that moment that it was very easy to say, "No." And I laughed at myself because my business was bootstrapped, it wasn't family money. I was eating what I grew, and $250 000 could have made a huge difference to my business. But I was able to sleep well that night. I thought the business owner would be mad at me, but he was actually really proud of me. He told me, "That's exactly what I want you here for: to keep us honest and make sure we're not making decisions that are just revenue-driven. We're making products that are supposed to help people, and as soon as that mission is in jeopardy, the money doesn't matter."'

In the socialised mind, our values are usually associated with what gets us safety and approval, rather than what helps us grow and develop. In the self-examining mind, we deliberately choose values to support our growth edge, values that help us to overcome our biggest fears and push us further towards a deeper level of integrity. In another example, Urs Karkoschka, Head of Human Performance Innovation at Novartis, recalled how he had unconsciously developed the value of harmony as a child. He said, 'I was the fourth child in my family, and my parents argued night and day. To survive in my family, I couldn't add any more pain, so I always tried to stay in the background and only do things that would create harmony, rather than adding oil to the fire.

'That desire is still very strong in me. It may be helpful in certain situations, but it has come at a cost. I will often give way to fear of disharmony and avoid difficult conversations that really need to happen, and in doing so I unintentionally break my precious value of integrity. I also have a tendency not to be honest with myself about my own needs in order to make everyone around me happy. I lose integrity with myself.'

To counteract this tendency, Urs has consciously cultivated the growth value of honesty. He has focused on developing the ability to have tough conversations and to assert his needs, even knowing it may come at the cost of disharmony or disapproval. This is the work of self-examining and of values-based leadership.

The question 'What is the talk you're trying to walk?' can be a useful litmus test to gauge whether a person is in the socialised or self-examining mind. By definition, a person stuck in the socialised mind struggles to consciously choose and live by his own values because he's subject to his need to be admired, liked and accepted by the group. To consciously and consistently choose to live one's values requires a well-developed self-examining mind.

David Tolman, General Counsel and Global Legal Head for Novartis Oncology, told me, 'There was a time in my career when I definitely had the addiction to looking good. And I look back and think, If I was trying to live my values instead of looking good, would I have made a different choice? The more aligned you are with your values, the less you care about how you look. You've lost that addiction; you're now much truer to what matters and in the end you're going to feel better.'

It has been our experience that by far that the biggest need in all organisations is to transition from socialised mind leadership to values-based, self-examining leadership, where leaders consciously choose their values and work to align and transform their behaviours with those values. As an illustration, when responding to the following three questions, it would be no exaggeration to say that less than 1 per cent of leaders have been able to answer them convincingly:

1. *What is the talk you consciously try to walk each day?* If it takes you more than a few seconds to start your answer, it is clearly a question that is not consciously informing your behaviour.

2. *When was the last time you had to overcome socialised mind fears (such as embarrassment, exclusion, upsetting others or being different) in order to walk your talk?* If it is not as recent as the past two weeks, you are not consciously walking your talk.

3. *When was the last time you failed to walk your talk, and do you know what drove your behaviour at the time?* If it is not as recent as the past two weeks, you are not consciously walking your talk.

(*Note:* The percentage of leaders who can answer these questions is substantially lower than the research on the percentage of the population at the self-authoring stage would suggest. In truth, this puzzled us, as we would have expected to see a closer correlation between the two. However, after much discussion with industry experts, including Robert Kegan's associates, we realised we are describing the self-authoring mind at an advanced stage. In this advanced stage, values are not only clear and self-confirmed, but also used as tools for vertical growth and transformation; they both stabilise and destabilise. They are in service of the development of refined awareness, as opposed to inner rules or edicts. This stage, which correlates with Cook-Greuter's stage 8, is moving closer to the self-transforming mind described below.)

The awakened mind

Kegan's highest stage of adult development is what he calls the 'self-transforming mind'. While rare, it can develop through the conscious inner work that occurs in the self-examining stage. In this stage, our sense of self is not tied to particular identities, values or roles. We develop an understanding that our awareness itself is closer to who we really are than our values.

Just as we differentiate between Kegan's term *self-authoring* and *self-examining*, we also speak of the *awakened mind* rather than the *self-transforming mind* when describing the highest level of development.

The awakened mind has the ability to see our ego at the subtlest levels, including our attachment to our values. We develop the capacity to 'make object' our most subtle assumptions and perceptions. It is, however, the values work at stage 4 that stabilises and settles the mind so that practices like mindfulness can reveal this deeper understanding and awareness. As the mindfulness saying goes, practising mindfulness without practising deep ethics and values is like rowing a boat still tied to the jetty. You're not going to get anywhere.

The awakened mind moves us beyond the potential psychological rigidity that can emerge from a self-examining mind, as we become attached to our specific interpretation of values and seek out reinforcement to warrant them. An awakened mind is able to determine whether our understanding of these values is still appropriate or whether the time has come to shed, include or transcend to new values or a new understanding of our values.

In an awakened mind, we are able to see our inner judge in all its forms, and to ignore or question it. For example, I might unconsciously think, *I should be more kind.* In a socialised mind, I would want to be more kind in order to be more liked and accepted. In a self-examining mind, I might agree with this inner judge because I value kindness and appreciate how it helps me overcome greed and fear. In an awakened mind, I can stop the process and ask, *Is that voice valid? Is it true?* That ability to fully question our own inner voice of authority and still feel inwardly safe and settled belongs to the realm of the self-awakened mind.

Achieving an awakened mind can be very liberating and rewarding. But trying to skip the work of stage 4, the self-examining mind, is not only a bad idea, it's impossible. The reality is we can't skip any stage, hence the need to call this a maturity model. We need to fully integrate one phase before moving to the next, to transcend each stage to continue the development process.

Two guiding principles can help us explore this final stage of development:

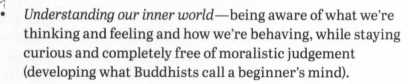

- *Understanding our inner world*—being aware of what we're thinking and feeling and how we're behaving, while staying curious and completely free of moralistic judgement (developing what Buddhists call a beginner's mind).

- *Transcending our mind's insistence on defining who we are and we are not*—practices such as meditation, being truly present to our senses in any given moment, connecting with nature and other consciousness-shifting practices can allow us to transcend our constant preoccupation with telling ourselves stories of who we are in relation to others and the world, weakening the hold of our ego-driven view of the world, with all of its fears and perceived threats.

An awakened mind is thus constantly open, aware and curious. It's less about learning than about unlearning and being in the present moment with objective consciousness. We become less fixed and rigid in our viewpoints and are able to embrace many different perspectives. Our security comes from our awareness itself, rather than our viewpoints, beliefs, and identifications or socialised mind preoccupations like the validation of others. We make peace with the impermanence and fluidity of life.

David Tolman, at Novartis, told me that the key to his own transformation has been non-defensiveness. 'Wrong perceptions lead to incorrect thinking and unnecessary suffering,' he explained. 'So I've learned to constantly ask myself the question, Are you sure? It's an invitation to question my assumptions and perceptions. Am I really seeing this accurately? What am I missing? And if I'm defensive, I'm not able to really see where I may be off and where I'm just protecting myself instead of being open to learning and growth.

'This process can be very confronting because we don't like to admit we've been wrong, especially when it's a perception we've had for a long time. Non-defensiveness and humility can be very freeing because they allow us to see things from a different angle.'

It should be noted that most of the time we're in transition between stages, behaving at different stages with different people. When we are genuinely self-aware, we pay attention to what is driving our actions or thoughts in any given circumstance. With this level of awareness, we can choose to deliberately let go of limiting perspectives, thoughts and actions.

The bottom line is that the more advanced our adult development, the less we are subject to our impulses and desires, our need for approval or to be good, right, superior or expert, even our need to self-define, and the more we are able to observe our preoccupations objectively and make wiser, more conscious choices. In effect, it's a self-awareness journey.

A self-examined life requires courage, but it's worth it

Living from the self-examining mind entails taking risks. For example, the mindset of a person in a socialised mind is, *I'll be honest to the degree that it's safe. I'm not going to be honest if I'll be ridiculed or even fired for it.* A person at the self-examining stage, while finding it extremely challenging, will follow their values even if it results in ridicule or getting fired.

As psychologist Abraham Maslow said, 'One can choose to go back towards safety or forward towards growth. Growth must be chosen again and again; fear must be overcome again and again.' It's a confronting process, but it's worth it. The more we exercise our ability to choose our own values and behaviours, the less fearful and the more confident we become. The ultimate result is more happiness and fulfilment.

In one study involving 5299 participants, researchers found that the stronger one's character, the more life satisfaction one felt.[4] A 'strong character' means consciously choosing and consistently living one's values. While this may seem self-evident, it's not obvious at all to the socialised mind. The socialised mind believes it's more important to win or maintain approval and be safe. In other words, a lot of energy and time are invested in image management, as opposed to values congruence.

The socialised mind depends on external validation for happiness. The self-examining mind understands that happiness is an inside job. As Harvard University researcher Shawn Achor concluded after a 12-year study on happiness, 'In reality, if I know everything about your external world, I can only predict 10 percent of your long-term happiness. 90 percent of long-term happiness is predicted by how your brain processes the world.'

We know from mindfulness practice that we become anxious when we don't follow our values. In a socialised mind, we are in a state of internal conflict, torn between our desire to fit in and our desire to choose our own path. We're torn between, *Should I follow the truth, or do whatever I need in order to look good and be accepted?* In mindfulness terms, this perpetual state of incongruence and dissonance is referred to simply as suffering.

The only way to feel internal congruence is to self-author our lives. The most effective method of doing this is to consciously choose values and align our behaviour with them. When we look at values from the socialised mind, our thought process is something like, *I need to follow good values to be a good citizen.* The self-examining mind thinks, *My self-worth is not dependent on how others see me. I want to follow my values so I can be more congruent and less reactive. I want to grow and overcome my biggest fears and avoidances.* Thus, the process of choosing and aligning with values is a recipe for internal harmony and happiness.

Anna Fillipsen heads People and Organisation for the Asia region of Novartis pharmaceutical company. She shared with me how living her value of authenticity has made her feel more alive in her work. 'In the corporate world it's easy to put on a poker face, and many people do it,' she said. 'We want to fit in, we don't want to show our vulnerabilities, for fear of being taken advantage of.

'Putting on a poker face makes it much easier to survive and not cause conflict. You can go through life without scratches. But in the process, you lose the essence of yourself. You start asking yourself, *Who am I?* Because it's when I show my authentic self that I feel most alive. That's the me I like. Without authenticity, I don't fully open myself up. I don't fully live. And ultimately I don't have the impact I want to have.

'That's the real problem with inauthenticity. It's not productive. We put all our energy into image management, rather than impact. It's about us looking good, rather than doing good. Image management adds a lot of stress and anxiety in our work because it's all about approval. It's about asking for confirmation that we are good enough, instead of putting that energy into helping others.'

In short, when we consciously choose our values and do the vertical growth work needed to live in congruence with them, we experience more health and wellbeing, happiness and fulfilment.

Having said this, it's also important to note that the process itself can be messy and scary. It can trigger significant discomfort as we shift from one level of development to the next, like a lobster shedding a shell to grow, with all the vulnerability that comes with it. As we shift from socialised mind to self-examining mind, we can look back on our lives and see the pain of depending on other people's approval.

While in a socialised mind, we usually don't even recognise this constant anxiety—it's just how life is. But as we release that well-protected ego structure and move into self-examining mind, we may experience moments of discomfort, grief, suffering or anxiety. This not something to be worried about, but is rather a healthy sign. Acknowledging and allowing grief or discomfort to flow through us is all part of the journey. Anna Fillipsen shared with me, 'In my transformational journey I have gone through prolonged periods of pain and feeling lost. I just see walls all around me. In that stage, it takes a lot of courage to break down your defences and get to the root of issues. But it's so rewarding once I have the breakthrough.'

Leadership and the self-examining mind

Leadership is the cornerstone of engagement. In fact, nothing else has statistical significance on engagement apart from the behaviour of leaders. Our Mindful Leader 360° assessment measures the impact of our seven mindful leadership practices on the variables of workplace engagement: leadership effectiveness, leadership trust and credibility, mental health and organisational trust. To complete the assessment, participants are given a list of questions on each leadership practice that ask them to rank their bosses on the seven practices. These seven practices are developing self-awareness, inspiring a mindful vision, leading from mindful values, skilful accountability, staying open and continually learning, empowering others and engaging the heart of those they lead. They are also given a list of questions to rank themselves on such measures as mental health and levels of engagement.

When these mindful leadership behaviours are applied, the results are tangible. According to our research since 2017, in addition to the engagement and mental health impact we mentioned in the Introduction, these practices have also been shown to boost leadership effectiveness by 46 per cent, leadership trust and credibility by 49 per cent and organisational trust by 35 per cent. In short, the more frequently leaders demonstrate the seven mindful leadership practices, the greater the impact on positive workplace attitudes of people in their workplaces.

Of course, when it comes to actually deliberately improving their leadership, the self-examining mind has a distinct advantage in that they have the capacity to consciously define development goals within the context of their principles and values, and move beyond fear. In his leadership classic *A Failure of Nerve: Leadership in the Age of Quick Fixes*, Edwin Friedman explains, 'When I fail to distinguish who I am from the organisation to which I belong, then I begin to identify more with the organisational fears and power structures than I do with my own principles and goals. As a consequence, I enable the organisation's most emotionally immature and pathological members to set the agenda, because they express their needs and fears more forcefully than I can my principles and goals.'

This is the difference between a socialised mind and a self-examining mind.

Caroline Barth, Chief Human Resources Officer for Lonza, a multinational chemicals and biotechology company, explained to me how she has grown as a leader by learning to be true to herself. Years ago an experience left her shocked to discover a big discrepancy between her personal values and her company culture. Although she felt a visceral unease, she let it slide and moved on. She shared how she has changed over time by learning to work within corporate culture but still living her own values. 'Five or ten years ago, I would have held back when I saw the reactions of people telling me, "We don't do that here." Now I enjoy experimenting. Instead of just caving, I'll say, "Well, I'm going to do that here and see what happens." I'm not afraid of the consequences. If they were to let me go for being too far outside of the corporate box, I would be okay with that, because I would realise we're not right for each other. It's more fulfilling for me to be true to myself.'

Victor Bultó, President of Novartis Innovative Medicines US, shared how self-awareness has helped him grow as a leader and stay true to his values. 'The more self-aware we are, the more objective we can be,' he suggested. 'And the more objective we are, the more choices we have. Leadership is all about making choices and helping others make choices. Without good self-awareness, our choices are going to be poor by definition. We will simply be living out scripts given to us by others and ruled by our own unconscious patterns and habits. In that state, our choices are not even our own, let alone wise.

'I've often fallen into the trap of rigidly clinging to my perspectives and beliefs. But I've learned that forming a strong opinion is probably one of the biggest barriers to true leadership. I have to be able to challenge and re-challenge my opinions and perspectives to adapt to change.'

When I asked Victor how his values have served his leadership day by day, he was quick to respond. 'They allow you to answer one question, and not 100 questions. As a leader, you're always pulled to where there's no clear answer. And trying to make up an answer to every single problem you encounter every day is an exhausting exercise. It's also very confusing to your team because they don't get a clear pattern or direction.

'So I see my values as an anchor. No matter what the problem is, I can always refer to my values, which provides a consistent framework for leadership. It saves tons of energy. And it also develops authenticity, because people see that you're not just making up answers as you go. You're consistent with something deeper.'

To lead effectively, it's critical that we live from the self-examining mind and become very clear on who we are, what we stand for, and the core values that govern our behaviour and decisions. We must cultivate the ability to withstand disapproval and stay true to our principles. This is how we self-author our lives and discover a much deeper congruence within ourselves.

3
How values help us grow

'Create a life that feels good on the inside, not one that just looks good on the outside.'

Anonymous

A cceptance and Commitment Therapy (ACT) defines values as, 'chosen concepts linked with patterns of action that provide a sense of meaning that can coordinate our behaviour over long timeframes. Examples of such patterns might be acting lovingly towards one's partner or being present with one's children. Values in this sense can never be fulfilled, satisfied or completed. Rather, they serve to give us purpose, intent or direction for each instance of behaviour.[9]'

We simplify the definition as follows: 'A virtue or value is a quality that, when cultivated, creates long-term connection, trust and harmony within us and in the environment or groups we live and work in.'

I emphasise *long-term* because sometimes following a value in the short term can be quite stressful. But if we follow it repeatedly, over time it develops deep trust and congruence within us. Ultimately, it gets us what we want, which is internal harmony as well as harmony in our families, teams, organisations and communities. Values help us achieve our highest potential.

Values, such as honesty, respect, curiosity, kindness, generosity and presence, were once expressed as 'virtues'. The philosopher Marsilio Ficino, the father of the Italian Renaissance, asserted, 'If you perfect one virtue, you perfect them all.' What Ficino understood is that the *process* of perfecting a virtue is what transforms our behaviour and cultivates the awareness and maturity required to master our mind, rather than the virtue itself. Virtues challenge the fears of the socialised mind, and the process of perfecting them is about overcoming our conditioned responses.

Values help us to be happier by cutting through our mind's conditioned responses to whatever we experience in life.

Avinash Potnis, Managing Director for the Pharma division of Novartis in Turkey, shared a powerful personal story of how developing his value of authenticity has been a huge factor in his rise to success. 'By authenticity I mean that I don't have to be anybody else,' he explained. 'I don't have to pretend or put on masks. I can just be myself. It's the only way I can connect with people.

'However, authenticity has not come easy for me. I have had to work on it. I came from a very small village in India. I was able to get a degree and enter the corporate world, but that wasn't enough. I was always trying to hide my humble roots and pretend to be someone I was not. This manifested as arrogance, though it was in fact deep insecurity. I was not really connecting with people, and I didn't understand why.

'My inauthenticity caught up with me in the summer of 1999, when I was at the pinnacle of my arrogance. I was called in to interview for a global position at Novartis. I had 16 interviews in two days. I felt confident that the position was mine—until my last interview, with the department head. Within five minutes of our interview he told me, 'You're not going to be part of my team.'

'"Why?" I asked. "You haven't even interviewed me."

'He answered directly. "I read the summary of each of your previous interviews. I fear that your internal growth is not where it should be in order to become a global leader."

'I came back to India shattered. I had no idea what had gone wrong. I was in complete denial, and I stayed in denial for at least six months. To drive it all home, in December of that year I was fired from Novartis. My wife wasn't working and our child was a year and a half old. We had five days to vacate our apartment, which Novartis had been paying for. It was brutal. To this day I have nightmares thinking about that period of my life.

'Sometimes it takes situations like this to wake us up. When I look back at the person I was before getting fired, I would not employ myself. I had no humility, and I was not being authentic.

'During this time I attended a seminar where the speaker did an exercise that ignited something in me. He showed us a clear glass of water and said, "This is your state of mind when you're born." He then put a drop of ink in the water, which became murky. He said, "This is the state of your mind now. All the open curiosity you had when you were born has now become preconceived ideas and the mask you wear for the world. The data in your mind is murkier still.

'To complete the exercise, he then added water one drop at a time and with each drop the water became clearer. "What this represents," he told us, "is that you have to deliberately work with your mind. You have to keep putting awareness (clear water) into it in order to clear your murky thoughts and beliefs."

'For the next two years I listened to thousands of audiotapes and read a couple of hundred books. About 18 months into the process, I started noticing how much my mind was opening up. My insecurities began disappearing and I began to live much more authentically than I was ever able to before. I realised that the world has space for everybody, and I don't have to be insecure at all. The moment that happened, I became a better contributor. I was okay within my skin, with my accent, my thoughts.

'When I tasted the freedom of authenticity, I wanted more. So I continued to cultivate this value in my life. Between 2002 and 2005 I was a project manager for a company in India. Our small team was able to accomplish amazing things. In 2005 Novartis called me back and rehired me. My first job was in the Philippines. Then, within just a couple of months, the regional head came to visit me from Germany and asked me to be the country head for the Philippines.

'Almost overnight I went from being a small project manager to a country head. This was all the result of the growth that came as I strived to become more authentic over the course of years.'

For Avinash, perfecting the one virtue of authenticity impacted every aspect of his career and life. Steven Baert, former Chief People Officer and Executive Committee Member of Novartis, shared with me how the process of consciously choosing his values has helped him overcome conditioned responses in his leadership. As he put it, 'When you try to change deeply embedded patterns, you'll always have a voice in the back of your mind that says, Go back to that comfortable road. You know how to drive that road. What are you doing out here in the jungle with a machete trying to create a new path, when you know there's already a very comfortable, well-beaten path?

'I had to lean into the fear that arose in me as I tried to change behaviours in me that weren't aligned with my values. At some point you realise your comfort zone is no longer attractive because you need to grow throughout your career. And although there is pain that comes with growth, it's also refreshing and liberating to realise you can choose new behaviours that serve you better.'

Values to increase engagement and commitment

In addition to transforming our behaviour, following values also makes us more engaged with and committed to our work. Jim Kouzes and Barry Posner performed a large study to gauge the relationship between living values and people's commitment to their work. They asked participants three questions:

1. How clear are you on the values of your organisation?

2. How clear are you on your personal values?

3. How committed do you feel to your work?

They mapped out the responses on the four quadrants of the matrix, as shown in figure 3.1.

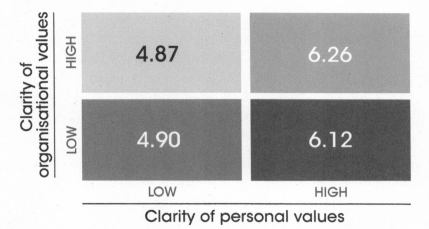

Figure 3.1: impact of values clarity on commitment

It should be no surprise that when people scored low on their personal values as well as on organisational values, their average commitment score was only 4.9 out of a possible seven points. Interestingly, those who reported having low clarity on personal values but high clarity on organisational values actually scored lower — an average of 4.87.

Even more interesting, however, is the engagement and commitment level of those with high levels of clarity on their personal values. As the figure shows, there was not much of a difference between those who were high on both personal and organisational values (6.26 average commitment score), and those who were high on personal values but low on organisational values (6.12 average commitment score).

What this shows is that having clarity on personal values impacts our engagement and commitment more than having clarity on organisational values. Those who are clear on personal values tend to be more engaged and committed regardless of organisational values. The bottom line is, when we're clear on our own values and we shape our life around them, we feel more alive and engaged in life in general.

Mimi Huizinga, Senior Vice President of Medical Affairs at ImmunoGen, explained to me how she sometimes uses numbness to escape from life. 'Numbness means you've built walls, so you're protecting yourself from agony. But in the process you're also blocking joy. When I'm numb, the organisational purpose doesn't energise or motivate me. I often feel like I want to sleep more. Everything is harder when I'm numb. And I'll often find myself doing unhelpful things to stay in numbness. It's amazing how many ways I can find to distract myself from doing the real development work.'

The key to pulling herself out of numbness, she realised, is to reconnect with her core value of curiosity. As she put it, 'When I'm feeling numb, it's coming from a place of frustration and exhaustion, rather than energising curiosity. I've been keeping a lot of feelings at bay. So when I can flip the switch into curiosity, I can reconnect with and explore my feelings, and reconnect with all of life. Through curiosity, I rediscover excitement and joy.'

This introspective work behind identifying one's values is key to becoming consciously developmental while fostering psychological wellbeing, both of which are foundational to achieving a self-examining or transformational mind. Clarifying one's values typically demands many iterations and requires us to ask at least four fundamental questions:

- *What really matters to me?* This is a very broad question. In an organisational context, it can be narrowed down to what really matters to me in this organisation or team, or as a leader.

- *What is life asking of me?* This question allows us to get outside our ego structure and let the more intuitive part of our self express itself.

- *Why is this important to me now?* It allows us to start honing in on what we practically wish to focus on in the present moment while anchored in a purposeful life.

- *Where is my life not working and what value/s could I adopt to help me grow and deal with this more constructively?* This helps us consider values from a growth perspective.

One of the primary reasons why individuals and organisations struggle to live according to wholesome values is that the concept of values is itself abstract. If values such as honesty, integrity and respect are simply abstract concepts, they can't be a living, breathing influence on our lives. They must be understood in tangible, measurable terms. Throughout the book we provide specific tools for translating values into measurable behaviours.

Quadrant 1: growth values

To best apply values in developing our leadership, the Mindful Leader Matrix provides a framework to render explicit what it means to have a rich and meaningful life at work, at home and in society. In quadrant 1, bottom right, of the matrix (see figure 3.2, overleaf), we seek to answer what is important to our growth. Values are at the core of this reflection.

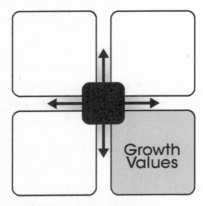

Figure 3.2: growth values (quadrant 1)

The most important leadership values

Obviously, you consciously choose the most important values to follow. To help you explore these values, it can be useful to examine the extensive research demonstrating which values best impact leadership effectiveness. The world's most popular leadership assessment tool is Kouzes and Posner's Leadership Practices Inventory, their 360° assessment. Their research shows that among the 30 statements by which they measure leadership, a lower than average score on 'Treats people with dignity and respect' has the most detrimental impact on leadership trust and credibility.

Essentially, this means that if we don't treat people with dignity and respect, we disqualify ourselves from being exceptionally good leaders. We also destroy any possibility of psychological safety, which is a prerequisite for high-performing, healthy teams with a growth mindset. According to Timothy Clark's extensive research, respect is absolutely essential for psychological safety.

The good news is that when we are mindful, feeling safe and present, treating others with dignity and respect is only natural. In reality, however, our shadow and the triggers in our increasingly challenging lives can move us away from these values, hence the need to make them explicit.

Kouzes and Posner conducted further research around the question, 'What do we most admire in leaders?' What qualities in leaders make us most willing to follow them? What characteristics do leaders need to be credible? A massive survey identified 225 leadership values and characteristics, which Kouzes and Posner refined to a top 20. They then conducted a survey six times over a 30-year time span in which they asked the more than 100 000 participants to choose the characteristics they most admired and were willing to follow in leaders.

Table 3.1 abridges the results of the most recent study, completed in 2017.

Table 3.1: characteristics of admired leaders

Norms	Characteristic	Norms	Characteristic
28	ambitious	84	honest
40	broad-minded	17	imaginative
23	caring	5	independent
66	competent	66	inspiring
31	cooperative	47	intelligent
22	courageous	18	loyal
39	dependable	17	mature
22	determined	10	self-controlled
35	fair-minded	32	straightforward
62	forward-looking	37	supportive

Source: James M. Kouzes, Barry Z. Posner. 2017. *The Leadership Challenge How to Make Extraordinary Things Happen in Organizations*. John Wiley & Sons Limited. Reproduced with permission of the Licensor through PLSclear.

As you can see, four qualities stand out from the rest, the highest being *honesty*, followed by *inspiring*, *competent* and *forward-looking*.

Honesty as a foundational value to a growth mindset

Honesty refers to being honest with both ourselves and others.

Honesty towards ourselves means we are committed to taking full accountability for our thoughts, emotions and actions. We are willing to be curious about what is happening inside ourselves, and to compassionately tell ourselves the unalloyed truth about what is going on and what our intentions are. It's a commitment to uncovering the truth, even if it's inconvenient or uncomfortable, and it's fundamental to growth.

Honesty towards others is also a challenging practice for all of us. We often don't give honest feedback, for example because we're afraid of ruining relationships or disengaging people. However, research from leadership experts Jack Zenger and Joseph Folkman shows that the more honest feedback a leader gives to their people, the more engaged they will be (see figure 3.3).

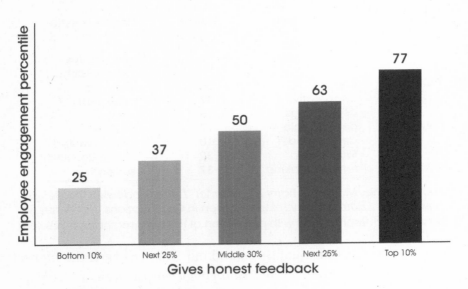

Figure 3.3: honest feedback

This accords with our experience over the years too. When working with leaders and teams we often hear the remark, 'We wish we knew where we stood with our boss.' Leaders will often withhold feedback for fear of upsetting people. The truth is, this actually damages relationships by undermining psychological safety. I saw this firsthand when working with a global executive team. I interviewed each team member at the request of the CEO, who wanted me to get to know his team and learn a little of how his leadership was going. Almost every one of his team said something like, 'Well, he's a great guy, but I never get any constructive or challenging feedback. Then when I hear that a person is leaving our executive team, I get really anxious and wonder if I'm next. I know I'm not perfect, so I'm losing trust in him, and it's making me anxious.'

Honest feedback matters, but it's also paradoxical. If we want people to feel psychologically safe with us, honest, sometimes uncomfortable, constructive feedback is part of the deal. Don't confuse psychological safety with being avoidant. Avoidance is a form of image management and is fear-based, not values-based. Behaviours driven by fear tend to generate more fear—the opposite of psychological safety.

We provide greater insights and discuss best practices on how to provide honest and respectful feedback in Part III. But for honesty to become truly refined and valuable, it must first be identified as a conscious value to cultivate.

Now let's take a closer look at how to choose your growth values.

4

Choose your growth values

'Yesterday I was clever, so I wanted to change the world.
Today I am wise, so I am changing myself.'

Rumi

As we have discussed, quadrant 1 in the Mindful Leader Matrix brings clarity to the values that help us grow. Growth values, which pull us in the direction of our conscious or best intentions, are distinguished from assumed or unconscious values handed down to us from our parents and society.

When we work with clients who are in the socialised mind, they are rarely able to express their values clearly. Or if they can, they typically share them as if they were a personal brand—principles they live by unquestioningly in all circumstances. Ironically, their values appear to be used as an image management tool, rather than as a daily growth practice. Growth values explicitly invite us to acknowledge the gap between our best intentions and our behaviour. They invite us to consider the most important qualities we need to develop in order to overcome the fears and attachments inhibiting our growth.

For example, we once introduced the matrix to a team whose leader was notoriously avoidant. He struggled to have tough conversations and hold people accountable, and this was common knowledge among his team. So when he initially chose the values of compassion and kindness, an almost audible groan passed through the room. It was obvious to all that these were not the areas in which he needed growth. For the team to function better, they would have preferred that he chose the values of honesty and accountability.

This team leader was using his values to further embed his avoidant tendencies. They concealed his shadow, whereas the growth values of honesty and accountability would invite him to explore and resolve his shadow.

On a personal level, if you struggle with impatience and anger and begin to acknowledge the negative impact this is having on your life and leadership, you might choose patience or kindness as a growth value. Or if you find yourself constantly avoiding conflict and you recognise the enormous cost this is having on your mental wellbeing and leadership, you might choose honesty as a growth value. (Interestingly, few of our new clients realise that conflict avoidance violates the values of integrity and honesty.)

To help individuals, teams and organisations define their growth values, we provide a long list of potential values and virtues and the development needs they meet in our digital program, *The Mindful Leader: Vertical Growth*. An initial brainstorm helps narrow things down. This exercise needs to be an inside-out rather than an outside-in job. To best navigate our lives in a rich and purposeful way requires that we move away from social desirability and image management to really listen to what our inner wisdom wishes to express.

Clarity around our growth values is critical to living a self-examined life. Given that our socialised mind and conditioned patterns can easily move us away from what we value most, these values will guide us as we navigate life and leadership.

In some cases, our values may already be well anchored, but this does not mean they will always show up when times get rough.

We can easily move away from these values when we feel threatened, leaving room for our shadows to slip in, as described in chapter 5. Our mind is often hijacked by our older mammalian brain, so our patterns to reduce discomfort or seek out short-term pleasure kick in. The more clarity we have on our growth values, the greater our immunity to moving away from them.

Find your growth edge

When it comes to personal development and behavioural change, there are three zones in which you can operate.

The first is the comfort zone, where you do things as you've always done them, out of habit, with no attempt to change or improve. You experience no growth in this zone, only stagnation.

Opposite the comfort zone is the terror zone, which can frighten you so much that you experience a fight, flight or freeze response. Your amygdala is so triggered that you are overwhelmed by fears and emotions. There is no growth in this zone because you are so shut down that you can't think clearly. Indeed, this zone can traumatise you.

Between these two zones is what we call the *growth edge*. You're pushing out of your comfort zone and into your terror zone, but not so far as to overwhelm you. You experience discomfort and anxiety, but it's manageable.

Steven Baert, formerly at Novartis, explained to me that the growth edge is where we consciously interrupt the conditioned patterns in which we've been trapped. As he put it, 'We are always creating a level of order for ourselves, and that order becomes our comfort zone. But it can be a dysfunctional order. We can be comfortable in patterns that don't serve us. So in order to grow again, first we have to disrupt our sense of order completely and move outside of our comfort zone. Then and only then can we build a new, more holistic, more functional order. But it's very painful to disrupt the order we create for ourselves.'

Interestingly, when we're in this growth zone, the discomfort we feel is often far more amplified than other people might see or realise. For example, one of my colleagues tended to avoid difficult conversations. As we began working on this, initially his conversations with me were very tentative. Out of fear of offending me, he struggled with being honest. He would deliver messages to me mildly and kindly, while being convinced that he was actually being very direct and tough. At one point he told me he thought he was being far too blunt and even rude.

I chuckled and assured him that he was doing a wonderful job of being both direct and considerate. From my perspective, he was just being honest in a respectful way, and it seemed very relaxed; from his perspective it felt extremely uncomfortable. He was pushing through some deep misperceptions of his own behaviour. This is growth work.

Isabel Matthews, Head of People and Organisation of the Global Drug Development division of Novartis, told me how hard she had been working on changing her pattern of avoidance and giving people clear and direct feedback. It had been challenging, though. 'When I hear my own voice, I sound like a monster. My head is telling me that my feedback is harsh, blunt and aggressive.' To feel more comfortable in the process, after giving feedback to people she would ask them, 'How does that feel for you? Because this is something I feel uncomfortable with, and I'm practising being clearer. Did that land like I'm a monster, or was it okay?'

Just as my colleague discovered, Isabel was surprised to hear that people actually prefer her directness because they know better what's expected of them.

When you start a new practice, you really need to push for that growth zone. You may feel like you're going too far, when you're actually being quite mild. A good sign you are really progressing with development practices is when people tell you that you're taking it a bit too far. In fact, 'going too far' is a rite of passage in vertical development work. If you are afraid of going too far, you will almost certainly never go far enough.

I enjoy swimming for exercise and was trying to improve my stroke so I could keep up with the faster swimmers in my group. A friend of mine is a swim coach so I had him look at my stroke and give me feedback.

He told me, 'When you're hitting the water, your arm is crossing your body too much. You're not bringing your hand to the center point, and that is twisting your body, so you're not as streamlined.' He taught me to throw my hand out farther in front of me. When I practised it, it felt like my hand was too far out, but he told me, 'That's perfect.'

This is how behavioural change feels. In our minds, we may be overcorrecting and taking things too far, when it's more likely that we're not pushing hard enough.

As with all learning and growth, the key is to practise persistently and be patient with ourselves. As Selina Short, at EY, put it, 'Part of me is always looking for those *ta-dah!* moments, when everything clicks and you're done, your patterns magically transformed. But it doesn't work that way. It has to be continual and you have to just stick with it.'

Gervais Tougas, at Novartis, added, 'When I apply transformational practices just once in a while, it's hard and clumsy. But when I consciously practise every day, things don't tend to build up and it gets easier and easier. I'm getting better at saying to myself, *You weren't as bad as last time, and you didn't take as long to correct. You'll do even better next time.*'

Places to explore growth values

Although any value we choose to develop can strengthen our mind and improve our life, particular values may help us grow more than others. The organisational development firm Human Synergistics uses a valuable tool called the 'Circumplex', which can help us hone in on the values we need most.

The Circumplex breaks down the factors underlying performance effectiveness (at individual, group and organisational levels) into 12 behaviours or styles. These styles are further grouped into three general clusters or zones:

1. **Aggressive/defensive styles** lead people to focus on their own needs at the expense of those of their group and organisation. This leads to stress, turnover and inconsistent performance.

2. **Passive/defensive styles** lead people to subordinate themselves to the organisation, stifle creativity and initiative, and allow the organisation to stagnate.

3. **Constructive styles** encourage the attainment of organisational goals through people development; promote teamwork and synergy; and enhance individual, group, and organisational adaptability and effectiveness.

Many of us (myself included) best fit into the first zone: our natural tendency is to be perfectionist, competitive, power-centric and oppositional. These leaders tend to care less about the feelings of others and more about outcomes. They can often railroad others in the pursuit of a goal. For us, the socialised mind values motivating our behaviour are power, status and winning.

Those in the second zone have a natural tendency to be more avoidant, dependent, conventional and focused on approval. They avoid tough conversations; they don't want to rock the boat; they want to be nice and fit in. The socialised mind values are job security, approval, comfort and belonging.

The third zone on the Circumplex represents an evolved, self-examining state. We develop with wholesome values such as respect, honesty, integrity, compassion, curiosity and generosity. I've never met anyone who belongs naturally in this zone; rather, these tendencies must be consciously cultivated.

As you're reading this, I'm guessing you know if you naturally tend more towards zones 1 or 2. This gives you a clue to the values that may counterbalance that tendency. For example, if you tend to default to zone 1, choosing the value of excellence or accountability may actually be counterproductive because it may drive more behaviour associated with this zone. However, the values of kindness and compassion will tend to balance out your natural zone 1 tendencies.

Conversely, if you tend toward zone 2 behaviours, the values of kindness and compassion may not be the most helpful. Instead, you may want to focus on courage or honesty—values that encourage you to stand up for yourself, be clear about your needs, challenge the system, take risks and confront harmful behaviour.

Michaela Wortley, Coaching, Teaming and Mediation Leader for the Oceania practice of the professional services organisation EY, defaults to zone 1. She is driven and a perfectionist. Although these can be valuable qualities, in her leadership they manifested in her being controlling, task-driven and uncaring. She told me, 'When things aren't going fast enough or how I want, I chime in with my viewpoint before others have a chance to speak. I can come across as very critical when I feel there's a better way or it's not good enough.'

To overcome her zone 1 tendencies, Michaela chose two deliberate practices. 'I set expectations and then step away and provide space for others to deliver, instead of being constantly there to control the process. The other thing I'm trying to do is to just be more caring. When someone delivers incomplete or substandard work, I ask questions like, "What's going on in your world?" That's a very different conversation from, "This isn't what I wanted." It's more caring.

'I'm genuinely a caring person, but I'm also very tough and driven, and too often the caring takes a back seat as the toughness takes priority. I have to manage that side of me and consciously cultivate my value of caring.'

When considering the values you want to cultivate in yourself, identify those that will make you a more well-rounded and flexible human being. Psychological flexibility is a sign of maturity; the more mature you are, the more flexible you are. You can be gentle and kind, as well as tough and direct.

James Skinner, at EY, shared with me why he focuses on values that are difficult for him to live by. 'The only way to understand the blind spots or competing commitments that may be holding you back from living truly congruently is to set a value and a behaviour that you'd like to live but for some reason struggle with. I look for the behaviours that cause me stress and frustration because of my inability to control them in certain situations. By putting my chosen values and behaviours into action and then reflecting on the feedback I receive, I get insights into what is holding me back.

'You're never going to learn anything by doing something you already find easy. You need to set yourself at something you find difficult. Only by going on that journey will you start to recognise what holds you back in any particular situation.'

I often compare values to a love story. They're a deep commitment, like a marriage. They're not something to be taken lightly, because using them to overcome fear and greed is a tough journey. The values need to be worth the struggle of suffering disapproval, rejection, potential job loss and the like.

Earlier Isabel Matthews, at Novartis, shared how she has struggled with giving people honest feedback and has therefore tended to avoid tough conversations. When we dug deeper, she discovered that she would often cover up this avoidance in the name of her value of fairness.

I asked her, 'Subconsciously, what were you worried would happen if you gave people honest feedback?'

She responded, 'I was worried that relationships would be completely broken, and therefore nobody would like me. So instead of holding people to account, I would compensate for them. I wanted to avoid conflict and create harmony in the team. So I would tell myself that my value of fairness was helping to create harmony. At the risk of being perceived as unfair, I would give people the benefit of the doubt and would not confront them when it needed to be done.

'It all really came down to my core fear: *Would I still be appreciated? Would I still be liked and loved?*'

Her conditioned response, based on her subconscious assumptions, was avoidance. To overcome this pattern, Isabel chose to work on the value of accountability. 'This is first about setting really clear expectations up front,' she explained. 'In the past I found that I couldn't hold people accountable because I hadn't set clear expectations. This means that I'm now more true to my value of fairness, because it's not fair to hold someone accountable to an unclear standard.

'It also means providing immediate feedback to team members when it needs to happen, instead of avoiding it. I can no longer tolerate poor performance or behaviour in the name of harmony. This is not being fair to the team.'

As it was for Isabel, choosing values-aligned behaviours can become obvious just by being open to growth and feedback. I arrived at my two core growth values through a determination to grow, and trying to understand where my socialised mind patterns were hijacking my happiness and inner wellbeing.

The first value I worked with consciously was honesty. I came to honesty when Russ Hudson, the Enneagram author and teacher, helped me fully realise the extent to which I was presenting an image for other people to see, and how it was based on a deep lack of self-worth. Russ put it beautifully, 'Michael, this image is designed to earn approval, admiration and love. But the best you will ever get is people loving the image, not you. You will never find the connection and acceptance you long for by investing in that image. It's not even who you are. And not only that, every time you invest in image management, you reaffirm that your real self is unworthy of acceptance and love.'

That was a wonderful but also very tough moment of truth for me. Thankfully, Russ delivered it to me with a lot of care and sensitivity. I dreaded asking, but knew I had to: 'What can I do to get out of this self-defeating pattern?'

He recommended that I practise complete honesty and transparency. Yet that was the very last thing I wanted to do. I was terrified of this because I was convinced that if I shared my whole self with people, they would reject me, and my worst fears would come true. I would look like a loser, not a winner. Which is why I now tell my clients, 'The more a values-based development practice scares you, the more likely it is to be exactly what you most need.'

It took me many years of practice, and a lot of very challenging moments, before honesty felt comfortable to me. In addition to becoming more courageous, self-aware and genuinely honest, to my astonishment and gratitude, Russ's suggested development practice delivered the greatest prize of all: I have gained a deep sense of self-acceptance. That is priceless.

The next growth value I chose to cultivate was kindness. Several years ago I was sitting with a mindfulness teacher who had noticed that I was resisting some of the kindness practices he had suggested for me. He asked me, 'What's it like to be in the company of someone who is genuinely kind? Not needy, not fake, but genuinely kind?'

I replied, 'When you're in their company, you feel like you've come home.'

My teacher smiled and nodded. I realised that's exactly what I would love to develop more of for myself and other people. And so began the next journey of development practices that I am still busy with today.

I've found that these two values—honesty and kindness—counterbalance each other beautifully. When I'm practising honesty without kindness, it can get a bit brutal and unfair at times. Kindness tempers honesty. But equally, kindness without honesty can turn very quickly into neediness and faking. Honesty balances that out.

Results, goals and strategies versus values

Some people struggle to understand the difference between results, goals and strategies as opposed to values and virtues. Values are human characteristics or qualities that produce trust, and connection, happiness and harmony, and that can be followed in *any* circumstance.

This is why, for example, we do not encourage people to list 'success' as a value. Success is a consequence of achieving goals, which are not values. Instead, we ask, 'What virtue or quality of mind would help you succeed?' Or if someone were to list 'family' as a value, we would invite them to consider the underlying value that family represents, such as care, acceptance or love.

Sheila Frame, at Amryt Pharma, is very much in touch with her core values, and they have a strong influence on her life. When I asked her what her core values were and how she arrived at them, she replied, 'Two of my strongest values are fairness and equality.

I grew up as the youngest of three children and the only girl in the family. My father was a bomber pilot in World War II, and because of that he was able to go to university.

'In his mind, only one kid from every family should go to university, and it certainly wasn't going to be a girl. It was hugely unfair to me. So after I graduated from high school, I put myself through university. I moved out and didn't even invite my parents to my university graduation. I ended up being the only one of my siblings who graduated from university. My oldest brother, who received all my father's support and was supposed to be the one to attend university, played pool and drank and bombed out.'

It's easy to see why Sheila feels so strongly about fairness and equality. These values were coming from past trauma and a need to correct past injustices. As she entered the corporate world, however, she quickly found that she had to be flexible in her application of those values. She experienced several situations in which she wanted to fight injustice, but strategically it wasn't the right approach. Over time she learned how to stay true to her core values while at the same time being flexible in their application. Otherwise her values would actually be a hindrance, rather than a help.

In Part II, we dive deeper into why values must be chosen from a growth intent, to reach a better version of ourselves, rather than to protect ourselves from past trauma.

As you ponder the values you want to cultivate in your life, consider the following questions:

- What value/s, if practised, would help me to grow and become more balanced and wise?

- What is waiting to emerge from me to unleash my growth edge?

- Who do I know that I admire, and what specific qualities or values in them do I admire?

- What kind of people do I want my children to become? What kind of values would I love them to display?

- What value do I secretly wish I was better at?

- What value that is important to me do I find the most challenging to master?

Map your vertical growth journey

1. If you want to try this online, visit mymatrix.themindfulleader.com and either create a Mindful Leader Matrix or log in to your existing account.

2. Think about the person, leader or parent you aspire to be, and consider the above questions to choose your growth values.

3. Use the 'My Values' section in the 'Growth Values' quadrant of your Mindful Leader Matrix to define your values.

Warning: You will be tempted to fill out the rest of your Mindful Leader Matrix, but I encourage you to read the chapter associated with each quadrant to be sure you are filling it out correctly. Once you've completed your first matrix, Part III of this book will help you create one for your team and organisation.

Statement of aspiration

The work on values typically allows us to develop a new narrative around what is important to us and what we consciously choose to move towards in support of our growth edge. This emerging narrative can be captured as a statement of aspiration.

For the brain to register a significant shift in mindset, it requires clarity and an emotional charge to best activate neuroplasticity in the brain. A value can create an emotional charge, but a short storyline can help provide a deeper and more meaningful connection to the chosen value or values. Writing out a statement of aspiration can provide this additional charge to best support our intent.

A powerful statement of aspiration brings the future state into the present moment, as the mind registers this as a new reality, which helps reinforce the committed action to be defined in the following section. It renders explicit your belief system and brings additional clarity to your values. When completed, the statements of aspiration serve as a guide to moving you in the future.

Growth values: integrity and courage

Statement of aspiration:

'All too often I have let myself and others down through trying to control others. I want to have the courage to empower people and the integrity and courage to follow through on this commitment. I know this will test my resolve and my fast-brain habits! I want my team to have the space to grow and flourish.'

Growth values: integrity and service

Statement of aspiration:

'When I consider all the gifts of my own life, I see they were supported by a spirit of service in those who care for me. It's time to return that support to those whose lives I touch. Without service, nothing really works. Positions of power are positive only if they are treated as positions of service.'

Growth values: fairness and care

Statement of aspiration:

'Because of my own insecurity around being liked, I have avoided addressing behaviours in others that are neither fair nor caring. I now see this is not aligned with my values and it's time for courage, as I want to truly master the living and leading of teams that share these values. We are all blind and unfair sometimes. I commit to being the leader who addresses these behaviours and who role models being accountable for them.'

Growth values: respect and integrity

Statement of aspiration:

'When I consider the most painful experiences of my life, many of them were associated with being treated without respect or integrity. Ironically, I can fall into the same trap. I want to master the practice of treating others with respect and integrity, so I can heal my own past around this. In many ways it is like a new language to me.'

Map your vertical growth journey

1. If you want to do this online, visit mymatrix.themindfulleader.com and either create a Mindful Leader Matrix or log in to your existing account.

2. Think about why your values mean so much to you and why they will help you grow.

3. Use the 'My Aspirational Statement' section in the 'Growth Values' quadrant of your Mindful Leader Matrix to compose your statement of aspiration.

5
Commit to action

*'The most difficult thing is the decision to act, the rest is
merely tenacity.'*
Amelia Earhart

T he basis of leadership is trust. In his book *The Speed of Trust*,
Stephen M. R. Covey explains, 'Trust always affects two
measurable outcomes: speed and cost. When trust goes down,
speed goes down and cost goes up. This creates a trust tax. When
trust goes up, speed goes up and cost goes down. This creates a trust
dividend. It's that simple, it's that predictable.'

Research shows that the two most important qualities for leaders
to develop are respect and honesty. Unfortunately, leaders often
don't live up to these values. The research firm Willis Towers Watson
surveyed 32 000 people in 26 markets and asked them to respond to
three statements. Table 5.1 (overleaf) charts what they discovered.

Table 5.1: Do we trust our leaders?

Statement assessed	Agree (%)
Senior leadership behaves consistently with the organisation's core values.	56
I believe the information that I receive from senior leadership.	54
My immediate manager acts in ways consistent with his or her words.	57

Source: Adapted from Willis Towers Watson, GWS Global Report 2016.

Another research study performed by DataPad involving 2100 respondents in the UK gauged how much employees trusted their leaders. The survey asked employees the same question on 'trust' and 'respect' in relation to their executive leadership, heads of department and immediate line managers: 999 people responded to the question on their CEOs; 1264 responded to the question on their immediate managers. Of those who responded to the question 'Do you trust and respect your CEO?', 30 per cent responded 'not at all' and another 39 per cent responded 'a little'. Immediate managers were trusted 'a lot' by only 48 per cent of those who responded and 'a little' by 36 per cent; 16 per cent of immediate managers were not trusted at all.[5]

It's actually quite shocking how low these numbers are. One of our favourite questions to ask our clients is, 'Do you think the leaders who score low are aware that people don't trust them?' Evidently, most leaders are not. As professor of psychology Dan Ariely says, 'Individuals are honest only to the extent that actually suits them, including their desire to please others.'

Clearly, we have work to do not only in defining our values, but in committing to actually practise them.

This chapter focuses on developing real leadership credibility by actually walking the talk, committing to action and being held accountable for what we commit to.

As we have established, values are far more than lofty, intangible ideals. When applied properly, they are living, breathing forces that direct our behaviour. Are *your* values a living practice? What practices do you use and what actions do you take daily to align with what you stand for? If you have to think about it, then it's clearly not actually living or operational in your life.

Here are a few questions to help you gauge whether or not you are walking your values talk in your life:

- How did your talk shape your behaviour (walk) over the past week?

- At any point, did you refer to the talk you're trying to walk in order to modify your behaviour?

- Can you describe a moment in the past two or three weeks when you had to actively work through fear, a loss of approval or a sense of embarrassment in order to walk your talk?

If you struggle to answer these questions—as most leaders do—there's a good chance that you're not clear on your 'talk' and that you have no aligned development practice or 'walk'. The result is a loss of trust and credibility among those you lead.

Philippe Deecke, the CFO of Lonza, a global contract development and manufacturing organisation for the pharma and biotec industries, identifies one of his core values to reinforce as 'jointly achieving lasting great things'. He admitted to me, however, that he contradicts this value by taking too long to have tough conversations. 'I probably err on the side of being too nice,' he conceded. 'I can make tough calls, but I try to find ways to get around them. I tend to want to develop people for too long because I believe in their goodness. But if I wait too long, then I become part of the issue.'

'So,' I probed, 'when you are not addressing bad behaviours or poor performance, then you are in direct opposition to your value of achieving great things together as a team. Because then the team suffers...'

'Yes, I agree,' he responded. 'And what's worse is that I then overcompensate by providing the answer or solution, rather than empowering my team.'

I asked him about his practice for having tough conversations and making tough calls in order to stay aligned with his value. 'It's involving people earlier with issues that impact their work,' he said. 'Sometimes I feel this need to be smarter than others, so I feel like I need to come up with a solution before I involve them. I end up involving people too late. So now I make a conscious effort to get people involved before it becomes a problem.'

Gervais Tougas, Head of the Chief Medical Office and Patient Safety Group at Novartis, described how his four core values of love, forgiveness, tolerance and compassion guide his behaviour. 'I used to think they didn't apply in my professional job,' he said. 'But I've realised that they are actually excellent frames of reference when I'm trying to deal with situations. So now I am very conscious about applying my values at work. Am I being compassionate? Am I being forgiving? Because it's a choice. When I'm feeling pulled by contrary feelings and behaviours, I keep reminding myself of my values and the person I want to be.

'Through mindfulness I've cultivated the ability to be more deliberate with my values. I can watch myself and say, "Whoa, back off. You're a loving, tolerant, forgiving, compassionate person. Not that angry guy who's about to behead somebody." I used to play ice hockey, and that competitive side of me can come out. And it can be tempting to say, That's just the way I am. Then I remind myself, No, I can choose to be the person I want to be.'

This is exactly what it means to 'self-examine'.

Four steps for taking conscious, committed action

In the upper right quadrant of the Mindful Leader Matrix we find the steps for behavioural change (see figure 5.1):

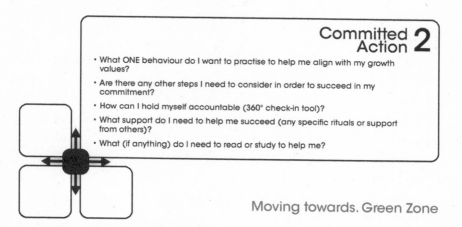

Figure 5.1: the Committed Action quadrant

Step 1: Identify your one big thing

It's pointless to choose values without a daily commitment to deliberately cultivating that value in action. People don't experience your aspirations—they experience your behaviour.

On making behavioural changes, Harvard's Robert Kegan and Lisa Lahey strongly recommend that instead of working on multiple changes at the same time, we always focus on what he calls your 'one big thing', or 'OBT'. This recommendation aligns completely with our 30 years of experience in this work. Less is most definitely more. Your OBT is the one big thing you want to change in your behaviour that will help you live your values and aspirations more consistently. By choosing your OBT, you are being deliberately conscious of your growth edge. You understand that this will likely lead to discomfort, but that it will be worth the effort. You are choosing to step out of your comfort zone.

Behaviour change is profoundly difficult. Lisa Lahey suggests it takes a minimum of 12 months to change one behaviour. If we choose more than one behaviour to change at a time, we're almost guaranteeing failure, because it confuses us and complicates the process. Think of this as applied to sports, like changing your swimming stroke, your golf swing or your running stride. In these examples, it's easy to see that it's impossible to focus on multiple changes at a time. You have to make one incremental change at a time.

Choosing a single, values-aligned behavioural change sounds simple enough. The truth is it's actually quite hard to do. One reason for this is that we are often blind to the truth about ourselves. If left to our own devices, we can choose behaviour changes that are misguided and counterproductive, which can both further entrench our fast-brain, moving-away tendencies and create more dysfunction in our relationships and teams.

Consider, for example, the avoidant boss who cultivates the value of kindness. He chooses as his behaviour change to 'listen to his team members more'. What is actually needed to improve his team's performance, however, is for him to get better at holding team members accountable.

Or consider the aggressive boss who cultivates the value of accountability and chooses the behaviour change to 'be clearer and more direct about holding team members accountable'. For her team, a more productive change may be to 'actively listen to team members to better understand their needs'.

Another reason why committing to OBT is challenging is because it is uncomfortable. Our fast brain seeks to avoid discomfort and to achieve short-term gratification. The mere idea of choosing a behaviour outside our usual repertoire will be unconsciously strongly resisted. We need to bring awareness to this discomfort and consciously choose with our slow brain what is truly best to support our growth, rather than please the ego structure that seeks validation or comfort.

To overcome these challenges and choose the most productive behavioural change for you, the best advice we can give you is to involve other people in order to gain greater objectivity. To become a more effective leader, ask your peers and colleagues, family and friends, and trusted mentors to help you identify your blind spots and your most important growth edge. In our digital training program, *Mindful Leader: How to Master Self-Awareness and Growth Mindset*, we almost always run leaders through our anonymous Mindful Leader 360° assessment, where their direct reports, peers and boss are able to give them a complete and objective picture of their real development needs.

Here's a useful hint: your OBT is probably the last thing you want to do, the thing you resist the most. That's where your socialised mind challenges lie. Paul Spittle, at Sanofi, explained, 'My OBT was given to me by my team: "Empowering others to challenge the status quo." I never would have come up with that in a million years. My team's feedback basically was, "You're really good at challenging the status quo yourself, but that doesn't always leave space for other people to do it. Create the space for and encourage other people to do it." I thought that was brilliant feedback. It's extremely difficult for me to do. And what's so beautiful about it is I never would have come up with it myself.'

Step 2: Identify additional skills you will need

Once you've chosen your OBT, your next step is to create the conditions for success. Ask yourself, *Are there any other steps I need to consider to help me succeed?* This step may include horizontal and vertical growth, the specific qualities, attributes, skills, competencies and behaviours you'll need to make it easier to succeed at your OBT.

For example, suppose you've chosen as your OBT 'Become more effective at holding team members accountable'. In this case, you may want to read books and attend seminars on improving your communication skills. Or if your OBT is 'Give more praise to team members', a critical supporting skill for you may be to become a better listener. By becoming a better listener, you get to know your team members more intimately, which in turn helps you to give them individualised recognition that really connects with their heart.

Step 3: Hold yourself accountable

The third step is holding yourself accountable for your OBT. There are many strategies and tools for doing so, which can include involving other people in holding you accountable.

Tracy Furey, Global Head of Communications and Engagement at Novartis Oncology, told me her OBT is 'To give timely and direct feedback in the moment, with added coaching and mentoring'. She needed help with this, she explained. 'I could feel myself over-indexing on the positive. Also, my team members told me I was too much about the positive, and not enough about growing individuals. And I realised that as a result my people weren't learning and growing as much as they could be.

'I struggled with it, because on the one hand I had a strong desire to help my people grow, but on the other hand I've always felt very uncomfortable with both giving and receiving constructive feedback. I worry about how I'm going to physically respond, like my neck gets red and I worry that people will see how uncomfortable I am. So I have all these fears wrapped up in it. But it's critical for me to overcome them and be better both for myself and for my team.'

To help her overcome these fears and hold herself accountable for her OBT, she established a ritual with her team members. Now, with every one-on-one meeting she has with a team member, she includes time for them to give and receive feedback.

Because we understand how vital accountability is to the process, we've built a 360° feedback tool, integrated with all our programs via our Awakened Mind mobile app, which makes the process simple and effective. The tool allows you to select a behaviour from a dropdown list or nominate your own behaviour you wish to change—your OBT. Through the app, people you select take 30 seconds to give you an assessment every two weeks on the progress they see in you for that particular behaviour. This creates a wonderful feedback loop to reinforce your OBT commitment until the behaviour becomes habitual. So if you're practising, you will start getting feedback and it will show your measurable progress, which keeps you motivated and inspired. If you're not practising, however, it will also hold you accountable.

Alexis Serlin, Head of the Asia Cluster at Novartis, who uses the 360° feedback tool on the app, shared with me how he gets the most out of it. 'The rating doesn't tell me much,' he admitted. 'But there is a place for open text. So I encourage my team members to use the open text and share examples of whenever I role model my OBT in a positive or negative way. It keeps the dialogue flowing, which is what we want.'

The prime conditions for growth involve both pressure and support, and you need both in your practice. When you hold yourself accountable, you create healthy pressure for change. But pressure without support can be demoralising, so the pressure must be balanced by support.

Step 4: Create support structures

Speaking of support, to achieve your OBT you must create support structures that help you succeed. These support structures include using rituals, involving other people and seeking out education opportunities.

Suppose your OBT is 'Be calm under pressure'. To help you with this, one daily ritual could include 10 to 20 minutes of meditation. Another ritual could include setting up a support group that meets every two weeks to discuss your OBT and practise it together.

You will want to involve other people to support you in your practice, such as trusted coaches and mentors, close friends, family or therapists.

Support can also include systems such as the previously described 360° feedback tool in our mobile app, or setting up reminders for yourself in your calendar or notepad. It can also include restructuring team meetings to best serve new behaviours, such as including a check-in moment for all to connect your OBT in a more meaningful way with team members.

Using the Mindful Leader Matrix

Now that you've seen the whole process of the right side of the Mindful Leader Matrix, it's time to complete your own Committed Action plan on mymatrix.themindfulleader.com, where you will also find real-life examples. Figures 5.2 and 5.3 are two hypothetical examples for your reference.

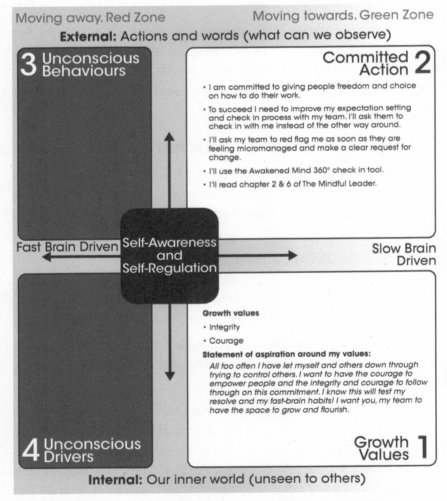

Figure 5.2: sample matrix (right side completed)

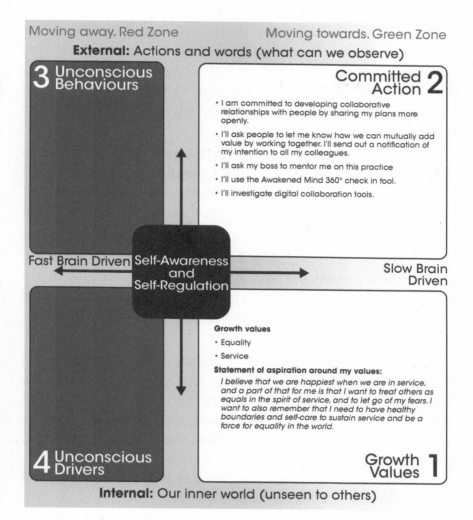

Figure 5.3: another sample matrix (right side completed)

The purpose of holding values is not to pretend that simply identifying with values alone makes us good people. Rather, it's to help us identify our values breaches, address them and change our behaviour to grow in the direction of our values. We don't choose growth values based on who we believe we already are. Rather, we choose them in areas where we see room for improvement.

By taking committed action in the direction of our values, we consciously move towards who we want to become, reducing the cognitive dissonance we feel and increasing our inner peace. Ultimately, the closer we align our behaviours with our values, the more we create a healthy environment in which all can grow and lead meaningful lives.

When I asked Gervais Tougas, at Novartis, why growth is so important for the success of leaders, he replied, 'I'm a biologist, so I view it this way: Life is growth. Life is an accumulation of events, of experience, of challenges. And if you don't define it as growth, then you might as well die.

'It's the same with leadership. Everything is in movement and you try to make it move in the right direction. I don't mean growth in a quantitative sense, but more in a qualitative sense. You try to make the flow easier, better, more constructive for everyone. It's adaptation in a mindful way.'

Now you have a solid overview of the Mindful Leader Matrix and the formal growth process it enables, we can dive deeper into the central role mindfulness plays. We can then look at the left side of the matrix, which deals with our misguided behaviours and the unconscious fears, attachments and assumptions that drive them. Our subconscious programming influences our behaviour in infinite unseen ways, so it's critical that we learn to dive deep into ourselves to understand what's driving our behaviour.

This is where mindfulness comes into play. Mindfulness is the primary method for becoming self-aware, even of the stuff we don't want to see inside ourselves yet that needs to be seen to enable us to get unstuck. Attempting personal growth without it is like trying to drive a car without fuel. Without mindfulness work, the Mindful Leader Matrix is incomplete at best. At worst, without the deeper insights that mindfulness can provide, our attempts to use the matrix can reinforce the very behaviours we're trying to correct.

In the next chapter we examine the role that mindfulness plays in the matrix and your personal development.

Map your vertical growth journey

1. If you want to do this online, visit mymatrix.themindfulleader .com and either create a Mindful Leader Matrix or log in to your existing account.

2. Think about the OBT and the supporting steps you could take to align with your growth values and aspirational statement, and fill out the 'Committed Action' quadrant of your Mindful Leader Matrix.

PART II

Developing self-awareness and resolving the shadow

6

The role of mindfulness in personal growth

'Just as a snake sheds its skin, we must shed our past over and over again.'
Buddha

In Part I, we discussed the value of moving towards what is important to us through clear growth values, developing a self-examined mind and unleashing our unique contribution. If it was this simple, many more of us would be there already. As we discussed in chapter 1, our older, fast brain is not wired to default to our growth values; it is wired to protect us in the short term. When working or living in challenging conditions or under perceived threats, our reactive brain kicks in and our noble intentions can easily fly out the window in the service of protecting us from emotional discomfort.

Training the mind to observe our mental and emotional patterns is therefore a great way to cultivate self-awareness and self-regulation, which are the cornerstone to sustainable vertical growth and values-based living. Mindfulness training has been around for millennia and has been popularised in recent decades as a powerful way to train the mind and mitigate the undesirable reactions of our unconscious mind.

We define mindfulness as maintaining an open-hearted awareness of our thoughts, emotions, bodily sensations and environment, paying attention in the present moment purposefully, warmheartedly and non-judgementally. It is experiencing and accepting the present moment—not how we want it to be, think it should be or perceive it to be, but as it really is. We can be mindful in any life situation—from driving, swimming or walking to leading, eating or writing.

Mindfulness is often confused with the practice of meditation alone. Meditation is simply the intensive practice of mindfulness for its own sake, just as a gym workout is intensive exercise for its own sake, though walking to the gym or work is also exercise. And just as if you go to the gym regularly, it becomes easier to walk up the hills to work, if you meditate regularly, it becomes easier to be mindful when it matters, such as when you are receiving tough feedback or someone is irritating you.

Through meditation and other mindfulness practices we become more aware of our habitual reactions, expand the gap between stimulus and response, and make wiser choices. We learn to recognise the inner motivations for our actions and become more honest and compassionate with ourselves. We learn to observe our perceptions, thoughts and judgements, rather than identifying with them and getting caught up in the mental stories we create. In short, we become profoundly self-aware, which is the key that unlocks the door to personal growth.

The greater our mindfulness, the greater our ability to self-regulate in real time. As Urs Karkoschka, at Novartis, describes it, 'For many years in the development of my self-awareness, the second element of self-regulation was missing. I thought that being self-aware was enough. I would be aware of my anger, for example, while still reacting to it. So my awareness was not complete, because I was not using it to mindfully manage my behaviour. Self-awareness is great, but if you can't mindfully self-regulate in the moment, it's not much use to you.'

Mindfulness training helps us develop:

- a mind that is not constantly reactive and is more interested in reality than the fantasy world the unmindful mind is constantly lost in. This leads to more slow-brain, wise choices and actions.

- the inner strength to feel and embrace uncomfortable feelings, instead of resisting, reacting and numbing. This develops a profoundly strong, peaceful mind and deep self-understanding and wisdom.

- the ability to see through false assumptions, beliefs and judgements. It can literally take you all the way to the highest level of adult growth and make your entire ego structure 'object'.

The research on mindfulness

One of the more fascinating discoveries the field of neuroscience has revealed about mindfulness is how it can literally change the structure and function of the brain, in the following ways:

- At the *cellular level*, meditation has been shown to change our brain chemistry by increasing the production of neurotransmitters and hormones associated with positive mood and feelings of relaxation and happiness.[6] The practice of meditation has also proven to decrease concentrations of stress hormones[7] and boost immune system function.[8]

- At the *structural level*, the practice of mindful meditation has proven to change the structure of no fewer than eight regions of the brain.[9] In the cortical regions of the brain, the home of cognition and executive function, researchers have demonstrated that meditation increases the volume and density of grey matter[10] (neurons) as well as the density

81

of white matter[11] (axons) that connect specific regions of the brain. These findings provide substantial evidence that meditation effectively 'rewires' the brain through the process of neuroplasticity.[12]

- At the *functional level*, the practice of meditation changes the pattern of electrical activity (neurons firing) observed in the brain.[13] Functionally speaking, this observation helps to explain the increases in self-awareness, attention control and emotional regulation, and better decision making that result after even brief periods of mindful meditation training.[14]

Taken together, these findings provide concrete evidence that mindful meditation training leads not only to subjective improvements in wellbeing, but to objective changes in the brain at cellular, structural and functional levels. There is clearly more than a placebo effect at play here. There's a cause-and-effect relationship between the practice of meditation and neuroplastic changes in the brain that lead to improvements in depressive symptoms, feelings of happiness and executive function.

Hundreds of research studies show that mindfulness practice provides the following additional benefits:

- stress and anxiety reduction
- improved cognitive skills
- enhanced creativity
- stronger relationships
- increased compassion
- increased insight
- increased mental wellbeing.

In his book *Neuro Dharma*, psychologist Rick Hanson cites many studies in support of the cognitive neuroscience behind mindfulness. One study showed that after just three days of mindfulness training, prefrontal regions behind the forehead exert more top-down control over the *posterior cingulate cortex* (PCC). The PCC is part of the default mode network that is active when we're lost in thought or caught up in 'self-referential processing' (for example, *Why did she look at me that way? What's wrong with me? What should I say next time?*). Consequently, greater control over the PCC means less habitual mind wandering and less preoccupation with oneself.

People who participate in mindfulness programs over the course of several months develop greater control over the amygdala, the source of our fight, flight or freeze response. They also grow more tissue in their hippocampus, a part of the brain that helps us learn from our experiences.

Experienced meditators, typically with years of daily practice, have thicker layers of neural tissue in their prefrontal cortex, which supports their executive function, such as planning and self-control. They also have more tissue in their insula, which is involved with self-awareness and empathy with others. Their *anterior cingulate cortex*, which helps us pay attention and stay on track with goals, is also strengthened. Furthermore, their *corpus callosum*, which connects the right and left hemispheres of the brain, also adds tissue, which suggests a greater integration of words and images, logic and intuition.

Clearly, mindfulness practice can have a profound effect on our ability to lead effectively and live a fuller, richer, more fulfilling life.

Zina Thaifa, a franchise head for Europe and Canada for Takeda Pharmaceuticals, shared with me how her mindfulness practice benefits her every day. 'When I practise mindfulness and take time to reflect it's much easier for me to behave according to my values. When I am unmindful, I will often work too much and not get enough sleep. This distracts me from my values. So I've learned to prioritise self-care and mindfulness, to reflect and re-energise.

'Mindfulness has also helped me to be much more curious, rather than judgemental, towards people. I really want to understand their story. And it's made me more curious about learning in general. So mindfulness is a way of being curious and learning, then refreshing yourself—becoming a better version of yourself.'

Brian Gladsden, at Novartis, added, 'There was a point in my career when my emotions were driving my actions too much. I was reactive, and it affected my judgement and damaged relationships. Mindfulness has given me space between my feelings and my reactions. I still have those triggers. They haven't gone away. The difference is that I now have space to choose how I want to respond, rather than just reacting or acting out.'

Two types of mindfulness training

One of the biggest misunderstandings about mindfulness is that it's primarily about calming the mind, 'finding our Zen'. The vast majority of the literature and training programs on mindfulness revolve around calming and stabilising the mind to increase our mental health and wellbeing.

The primary meditation technique for calming meditation is focusing on an *object of attention* or singular point of concentration. This usually means focusing our attention on the breath, which concentrates our mind on the present moment. If the breath is not a comfortable place to bring our attention to, the practitioner can use other objects of attention, like hands or body posture or external objects of attention such as sounds or images. If we're experiencing stress, boredom, anxiety or any other distraction, we keep coming back to our object of attention and training the mind to concentrate, settle and find balance.

This is clearly a very important part of mindfulness. It is not the full story, however. We've met many people who have practised meditation for years yet are still quite anxious and emotionally challenged. Their meditation practice may settle them in the moment, but it does not help them to achieve deep transformation.

This was my experience for my first 10 years of meditation. I would be a mess emotionally, so I would meditate. And I would calm my mind and gain a brief respite from my inner turmoil, but the causes of my emotional turmoil remained hidden as I focused on my breath. Despite my regular meditation practice, I wasn't seeing and dealing with what was under the surface and my own vertical growth was stalled.

This is why we need a second type of mindfulness practice that is oriented towards insight and development. The goal of developmental mindfulness is shadow awareness and resolution, developing distress tolerance, psychological integration and flexibility. Instead of escaping our inner baggage through meditation, it's about curiously and compassionately digging deeper into it, exploring it, embracing it and ultimately resolving it. It's about making object to us the unconscious patterns of feelings, perceptions and thoughts to which we've been subject. It's vertical growth in action.

In developmental meditation, we may start by focusing our attention on the breath to settle the mind. but then, invariably, something—pain, sadness, anxiety or some other emotion—will arise in us. This then becomes what we focus on. We track our experience mindfully and explore the feelings that arise. We don't repress anything or avoid it by just focusing on the breath.

The difference between calming and developmental mindfulness was vividly displayed in the example of one of my clients, an executive at a media company. She was crushed when she received poor scores on a 360° leadership assessment for the component 'Empowers people to grow and deliver their best work'. Another consultant recommended that she attend an online program on how to empower people.

While she was focused on horizontal development (the skillset of empowerment) I was more interested in vertical exploration— digging deeper into her psychology to discover the subconscious patterns behind her behaviour.

I asked her, 'Why do you think you micromanage others?'

'I'm not sure,' was her response.

I was grateful it wasn't 'I don't micromanage people'. All too often new clients are so heavily defensive and numb they cannot see or own their moving-away behaviours (the left side of the matrix).

After more exploration I asked, 'How long have you felt the need to be fully in control of the people in your life?'

Following some more conversation and coaching, she eventually described how in her childhood her parents had divorced and her world had become unstable and challenging. Not having control over important people she depended on had resulted in loss and pain. Tragically, at some level she even felt responsible for the divorce, which is a not uncommon reaction in children.

Her unconscious, core assumption creating the behaviour of micromanaging was that she needed to stay in control of those who could potentially let her down, and that controlling others was even good for them.

She was now conscious of the core reason why she was micro-managing, but she still had to deal with the behaviour. I told her, 'When you empower people and give them choice, your past wounding and fears will be aroused. When that happens, the first thing you need to do is ground yourself. Take a deep breath and mindfully feel and accept the emotional discomfort in your body. When you notice the urge to again start telling them how to do things, mindfully feel into the anxiety, keep breathing and just notice it and accept it without reacting to it.' This is not easy, and of course it requires developmental mindfulness training.

Critically, developmental mindfulness training enables us to feel and accept emotional pain without needing to avoid it or escape it. It is exactly this escaping or numbing reactivity to emotional pain that propels us into dysfunctional behaviours.

'People will make mistakes,' I explained, 'especially if they aren't used to being empowered. Once again, mindfully notice the fear and anxiety (make it object) instead of reacting to it and triggering old, protective patterns that don't serve you anymore. Then gently recommit to your practice.'

Although this created distress for her, she was able to mindfully stay grounded in awareness of her body and stay true to her values and her committed action of empowering others while being able to tolerate the distress. She was eventually able to break the pattern of micromanaging, team performance improved and her career got back on track. The self-awareness and inner emotional strength she gained in the process impacted every area of her leadership and her relationships. It was literally life changing.

Mindfulness and the Mindful Leader Matrix

Let's analyse her story through the lens of the Mindful Leader Matrix (see figure 6.1, overleaf).

In quadrant 1 was her value of *respect*. However, in quadrant 4 she had a lot of *unconscious fear*, *attachment* and *assumptions* from her childhood, resulting in a fixated need for *control*. This was triggering her unconscious behaviour of micromanaging in quadrant 3. When she was delegating tasks, her fast brain would take over and she would go into habitual control mode.

She needed some way to stop the pattern and cultivate slow-brain responses in alignment with her value of respect, in this case respecting her direct report's need for growth and trust. Using mindfulness, she was first able to notice (make object) her fears and old conditioning in quadrant 4, regulate the impulses to move into controlling behaviour (quadrant 3), remember her values-aligned commitment or OBT (quadrant 2), then accept her challenging feelings and still move towards her values and aspirations by actually empowering others (that is, the talk she wanted to walk as a leader and as a human being).

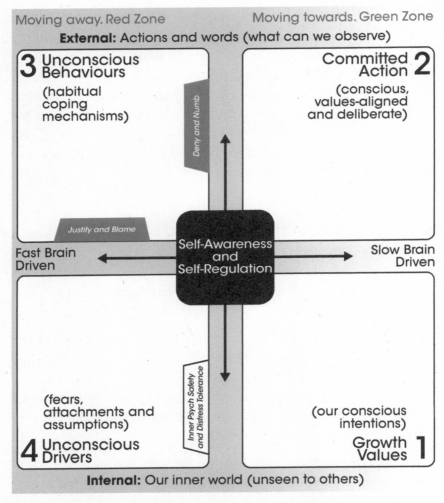

Figure 6.1: applying mindfulness to the matrix

Without the self-awareness that mindfulness can give us, all efforts to change our behaviour are much more challenging. Through mindfulness we can better observe our underlying conditioning and the emotional avoidance creating poor behaviour, then self-regulate in real time to consciously choose values-aligned behaviours.

Anna Fillipsen, at Novartis, explained to me how this works for her. 'There are times during conflicts when I feel my stomach churning and my body is like a tiger ready to pounce. When I'm mindful, in the heat of these moments, I can pause, notice the emotional turmoil and consider, Okay, how do I want to handle this? I remind myself that no one else is responsible for my emotional triggers, so I'm not blaming anyone for my strong feelings. I breathe and mindfully accept the feelings, which very quickly settles that inner tiger, then I can redirect my energy in a way that is more balanced and conscious.'

Lonza's Philippe Deecke added, 'Mindfulness helps me to view myself and situations from the outside and to reflect on my behaviour. It's about noticing what's happening within myself and exploring my reactions. *Why am I feeling this way? Why did I react that way?* It's only when I can truly understand myself that I can transform myself.'

Mindfulness cultivates distress tolerance

Mindfulness and the Mindful Leader Matrix give us powerful tools and a process for dealing with difficult emotions. We all experience both pleasant emotions, such as love, joy and comfort, as well as unpleasant emotions, such as fear, sadness, anger and shame. Because we haven't trained ourselves to accept difficult emotions, our immediate instinct is to do everything we can to make those emotions go away. We have a fast-brain response to seek immediate relief from the emotional pain.

Psychologist Susan David conducted a survey of more than 70000 people and found that 'a third of us either judge ourselves for having so-called "bad emotions", like sadness, anger or even grief, or we actively try to push aside these feelings.'[15] Our two most common avoidance techniques are numbing and denial. While avoidance may give us an immediate reward, it's very damaging to our long-term mental and emotional wellbeing, as well as our psychological flexibility.

Psychologists refer to this avoidance as 'distress intolerance', which is defined as the 'perceived inability to fully experience unpleasant, aversive or uncomfortable emotions, and is accompanied by a desperate need to escape the uncomfortable emotions'.[16]

Using developmental mindfulness, we can train the mind to stay present, curious, balanced, aware and connected—not just when we feel good, but especially when we feel discomfort. Research shows that heightening our present-moment awareness increases our emotional distress tolerance, which in turn decreases our chances of reacting negatively to emotional discomfort.[17]

When not pursuing avoidance behaviours, we spend excessive amounts of time ruminating on how to escape these emotions; we are fused to them, as if by spinning the hamster wheel some more, we can miraculously find a way out of our discomfort. The irony is that we are often simply feeding the beast. Ruminating is like a glitch in our software that keeps us stuck in our emotions, turning our stories upside down and inside out to figure a way out of the ongoing discomforts associated with the person or situation at hand.

In this process, we unwittingly embed the idea that our emotional wellbeing is dependent on others, or on the ideal external conditions, which enhances our anxiety and delusion. Mindfulness training teaches us over and over again that we have agency over our emotional world. But as long as we believe others are the cause of our emotional pain, we fixate and ruminate on all the wrong solutions. And we arrest our potential for compassionate accountability and vertical growth.

Psychologist Rick Hanson points out, 'The two fundamental cornerstones of unhappiness, depression and anxiety are distress intolerance and negative rumination.' In other words, the less tolerance we have for distress, the more inclined we are to kick into fast-brain behaviours. And the more we do this, the more limited we are, the less we can grow and the less aligned we are with our deepest aspirations.

We learn from ACT therapy that, 'once we've developed unhelpful ways to escape our emotions, we'll keep using them unless we push ourselves to change them by feeling and accepting them and still following our values'.[18] This is why identifying and cultivating values, alongside the ability to mindfully self-regulate, even in distress, is so fundamental to growth.

In quadrant 3 of the matrix we find all our misguided and limiting behaviours that prevent us from fully living our quadrant 1 values. In order to change our behaviours to align them with our values, we have to dive deep into quadrant 4 of the matrix—all our hidden conditioning that influences our choices and behaviour without our conscious awareness.

Taking ownership for our behaviour can be very challenging, however. In fact, we have become very adept at using the first line of defence, numbness and denial, as a means to escape looking at our unconscious behaviours in quadrant 3. If we then move beyond the second line of defence, our justifications and blame of others, we start uncovering quadrant 4 and the source of our moving-away behaviour. This too can be very emotionally challenging. It takes support, courage, awareness and a commitment to the truth.

The process of mindfully accepting and feeling painful emotions without reacting to them or trying to escape them cultivates distress tolerance. Accepting and feeling painful emotions usually means labelling what is showing up—be it fear, sadness, frustration, anger or any other combination of emotions you are aware of—then being aware, accepting and embracing the sensations emerging in your body, such as a tightness in your chest or belly, sweaty hands or a tight jaw. Observing the kinds of stories or narratives that show up in your mind is also extremely helpful. Neuroscience calls this 'metacognition'. It's the process by which we make our thoughts and feelings *object* to us, rather than being *subject* to them. We explore this in the next chapter.

Susan David tells us, 'Research on emotional suppression shows that when emotions are pushed aside or ignored, they get stronger. Psychologists call this amplification. Like that delicious chocolate cake in the refrigerator—the more you try to ignore it, the greater its hold on you. You might think you're in control of unwanted emotions when you ignore them, but in fact they control you. Internal pain always comes out.'

She adds a critical point: 'Emotions are data, they are not directives. Our emotions contain flashing lights to things that we care about. We tend not to feel strong emotion to stuff that doesn't mean anything in our worlds. If you feel rage when you read the news, that rage is a signpost, perhaps, that you value equity and fairness—and an opportunity to take active steps to shape your life in that direction. When we are open to the difficult emotions, we are able to generate responses that are values-aligned.'[19]

However, we tend to unconsciously allow emotions to become directives. For example, we feel angry, then we immediately react to that anger and act out in ways that violate our values. This is the fast-brain response to emotions. The slow-brain response is to view our emotions as data, accept them without reacting to them, and explore them to discover what they're telling us before we take action.

As simple as it sounds, accepting and exploring our painful emotions can be one of the most difficult things we can do, as our fast brain and ego structure cries out to fix the pain with short-term solutions.

I was once coaching a client around emotions. She told me, 'I'm feeling really sad.'

I asked her, 'What would happen if you just felt sadness?'

Her first response was, 'I'll get lost in it forever.'

'Oh,' I said jokingly, 'so you believe in permanence? You believe feelings last forever?'

I then asked her, 'What do you do to make the sadness go away?'

In her case, it boiled down to workaholism. Whenever she felt sad, she would throw herself into her work and work even harder. While it may look productive from the outside looking in, the reality is she is avoiding her emotions. So not only is she not dealing with or learning from the emotions, but she is also creating more long-term problems for herself.

When we see that emotional pain is impermanent and can be located in a specific part of our body, we can be less freaked out by it and realise that it can be observed, acknowledged, allowed to move through our body and, with practice, be resolved. When we recognise that pleasure, too, is impermanent, we can cling less to it. This is the biggest gift a cultivated mindfulness practice can give you: the experiential knowledge of this truth. From that knowing, we find a solid, balanced place in which to live.

I had a similar conversation with Brian Gladsden. He was telling me about the tension he felt constantly in his body, like a knot of fear in his system. I asked him, 'What's your relationship with that feeling?'

'I'm trying to work it out,' he said.

'So you can get rid of it?' I asked.

'Yes.' His thinking was essentially that if he could intellectually figure out the cause of his tension, he could then make the tension go away. It was all resistance. At no point was he relaxing and allowing it in. And since he hated the feeling, he was constantly reacting to it and acting out in his life. In short, he was creating more suffering in his life than the actual feeling itself. I've fallen into this trap many times in my life too.

'The key,' I explained, 'is to embrace the feeling without the agenda of getting rid of it.' Impermanence is a fact of life, and we know feelings don't last forever—they come and go. Resisting them does nothing but make them worse and make them last longer. The most skilful way to deal with difficult feelings is to be non-judgemental when they show up, be curious and kind towards yourself, relax and feel them. Let them be as they are, without adding mental stories to them.

With mindfulness practice over time, Brian has cultivated more distress tolerance. He told me, 'In the past, as soon as I felt something uncomfortable, I wanted to push it away. And that would usually come in the form of a negative reaction, such as barking at someone. So I would take my emotions out on others. Mindfulness practice has given me a much higher level of comfort to sit with painful and uncomfortable feelings. It's like being able to hold your hand to the flame. It's made a world of difference in my work as a leader. Instead of being emotionally reactive, I can take more time with issues and make better decisions.'

Reacting to our emotions puts us in a fast-brain state where we are neither thinking clearly nor acting consciously. With mindfulness, we can regain access to our slow-brain state while completely accepting our emotions. And in this state, we can then start digging beneath the surface to discover the source of our feelings and gain a deeper understanding of ourselves. This is the work of quadrant 4 in the matrix, which is facilitated by a mindfulness practice.

We further address the underlying causes of these avoidance and ruminating behaviours in chapters 7 to 9 as we dive deep into the notion of our shadow, which helps us understand the underlying fears, attachments and assumptions that support these unhelpful behaviours on the left side of the Mindful Leader Matrix.

7

How to practise self-awareness

'At the center of your being you have the answer; you know who you are and you know what you want.'

Lao Tzu

W e know from extensive research that self-awareness is the most important of all leadership skills. It's the skill that helps us interrupt the fast-brain habits that take us away from our values. It's what gives us the ability to manage the physical and emotional discomfort that comes from interrupting those habits. It unleashes us from our unseen limiting and destructive assumptions, thoughts and perceptions, and allows us to access our best self in times of pressure and stress.

Surprisingly, though, very few people know how to practically cultivate self-awareness. This is illustrated when we ask people a simple question: 'If you were to practise self-awareness right now, what exactly would you do?'

We get all kinds of responses to this question, ranging from being aware of your impact on others, to thinking about your habits, asking for feedback, even following your breathing. But these answers miss the mark.

To be self-aware is to be mindful and conscious of what is going on inside us, then learning how to manage our experiences and habits to act more clearly, deliberately and wisely in real time, not after we have acted, when it's too late. In other words, we radically increase our ability to be driven more by our slow-pathway brain in the moment. This is what we call real-time self-awareness—the kind of self-awareness that is available to us in any given moment, which in turn allows us to regulate our thoughts, intentions, actions and reactions wisely. This is why we place self-awareness and self-regulation at the centre of the Mindful Leader Matrix.

The four foundations of mindfulness

Awareness is paying attention. If we're not paying attention to something, we lose awareness of it. Mindfulness training is about becoming continuously attentive and aware of our experience.

To be self-aware means directing trained attention to what is going on inside us. But what exactly are we paying attention to? From mindfulness we learn that there are four aspects or realms of the self of which we can be aware. These are referred to as the 'four foundations of mindfulness':

1. **Mindfulness of the body/senses.** This means being present to our internal physical sensations as we interact with our environment. It is the most widely understood of the four foundations, and most mindfulness training, especially in beginner programs, focuses on mindfulness of breathing and the body.

2. **Mindfulness of feeling tone.** All our lived experiences can be classified as pleasant, unpleasant or neutral. These three 'feeling tones' are inherent in everything we experience. Through mindfulness we look more closely at our relationship with our fast-brain reactions to these experiences. In the fast brain, we naturally seek to avoid

the unpleasant, embrace the pleasant and generally pay little attention to the neutral. Bringing mindful awareness to our default fast-brain reactions is the first step in interrupting our conditioned responses to our experiences, and developing inner strength, empathy and connectedness. For example, by learning to stop running away from uncomfortable emotions through numbing, repressing or acting out, we develop maturity and deepen our integrity.

3. **Mindfulness of thoughts.** When we are unmindful, we associate and identify ourselves with our thoughts. Entranced by and subject to our own minds, we believe our thoughts represent objective truths (even though most of them are subjective assumptions and imagination). If our thinking is challenged by others, we feel personally challenged and quickly move to defend ourselves or rationalise. Mindfulness helps us to become more objective, less attached and more rational in our thinking. It helps us to stop defending our thoughts or ideas, which in turn allows us to truly test our thinking and discover new ways of thinking.

4. **Mindfulness of the way we make meaning.** Our interpretations and the conclusions we draw from life experiences and what things mean are based on fundamental assumptions. Not only do we usually not question these assumptions, but often we're not even aware of them. The fourth foundation is being aware of all the unconscious conditioning we're subject to that validates our prejudices and worldview. It's being mindful of our deeply held views, set ideas and unconscious biases—all the ways we filter reality. Mindfulness allows us to see through our fixed views, to let go of old prejudices and unhelpful, embedded beliefs (such as 'I am not good enough').

Once we become mindful of these four foundations, we are no longer possessed by them or pushed around helplessly by them. They become object to us.

I have studied and practised the four foundations for nearly two decades now. I regard this study and practice as more advanced, complete, refined and worthy of lifelong cultivation than anything else I have ever been exposed to through my many years of inner work and leadership work, and they perfectly align with and complement the Mindful Leader Matrix.

The four foundations of mindfulness are the master key to liberating us from the incessant push and pull of our physical sensations, emotions and thoughts. They are also why we spent an extraordinary amount of time and effort developing a comprehensive training resource on all four foundations through our mobile app—one of the resources accompanying the online course The *Mindful Leader: Vertical Growth*.

Mindfulness, in particular the developmental style of mindfulness practice, answers the question of how to be self-aware. The only way we can become self-aware in real time is to be aware of our body, our feelings and emotions, our thoughts, perceptions and deeply held views.

Without mindfulness, it's impossible to develop enough self-awareness to reliably transform our behaviour. The four foundations of mindfulness, then, are the practical application of self-awareness. If someone were to instruct you to 'be self-aware right now', you would first need to tune in to one of the foundations.

The first foundation of mindfulness: The body

Mindful meditation is often presented as a spiritual activity, but it is really a physical activity. When we get lost in the 'there and then' in our minds, we lose our felt connection with the body in the here and now. The body is always in the present. The more embodied we are, the more present and aware we are. It's really that simple.

The body includes all five physical senses: seeing, hearing, smelling, tasting and touching. Mindfulness of the body includes the whole package of living within the physical world, of being fully present to this world and the people within it, rather than being lost in the isolation of our minds. Mindfulness of the body is about feeling ourselves as a body within this physical world, rather than imagining ourselves as a dream figure in our own fantasy.

When we're grounded in the body, we find that our mind and emotions naturally self-regulate. When we're lost in our dreams, we find ourselves swept along by feelings and thoughts that are disconnected from our reality. But when we cultivate the habit of being simply present within and as our body, then we find our emotions and thoughts stabilise. We're quite literally grounded. In this state, we can deal with whatever challenges arise in the present without being knocked off balance by our thoughts and feelings or being lost in the past and future. This is why you'll find we dedicate so much mindfulness training on body awareness in the bonus resources accompanying our programs.

Gervais Tougas, at Novartis, explained how this works for him. 'I'm a very visceral person,' he told me. 'I feel it when things are right or wrong. Emotions are physical. I feel every emotion in my body. For example, when I get angry I feel it at the base of my hairline and in the back of my neck.

'In the past, whenever I would feel this edginess, I would tend to react and misbehave, but now when I feel that in my body I pause and reflect, *Before you say something now, can you articulate why you're feeling like this?* This puts me in tune with my body and emotions. It helps me to see things more clearly because I feel them in my body before I see them in my mind.'

A colleague at Novartis, Urs Karkoschka, added, 'The body never lies. Whenever I feel strong emotions, such as anger or frustration, I try to bring curiosity to those feelings. *What is really happening in me, and why?* That wonderful pause between stimulus and response allows me to respond consciously, rather than to react on autopilot. And that is enabled by being mindful of the feelings I experience in my body.'

Isabel Matthews, also at Novartis, recalled how for years she felt disconnected from her body and emotions. 'Before practising mindfulness I wasn't in tune with how I was feeling at all,' she conceded. 'And when I did feel emotions, I didn't connect them to situations or behaviour. I just thought I was having a bad day, but there was no understanding of why I was feeling that way.'

'With mindfulness practice I've recognised that my body is like an antenna. I can tune into it and know exactly what I'm feeling and why. Then I can consciously choose to face it, rather than run away from it by numbing, as I've so often done throughout my life.'

When practising mindfulness of the body, we're looking for a sense of acceptance in the body. This means we don't deny the discomfort we feel; rather, we accept any sense of tension or discomfort and relax into it. As we relax, we become more sensitive to what is happening in the body, and this is the aim of our practice. We're not trying to find something; we're trying to actually experience what's already happening at more profound levels.

The second foundation of mindfulness: Feeling tone

As already noted, in the context of mindfulness our experience of reality can fall into one of three classes or 'feeling tones': pleasant, unpleasant or neutral. Eating your favourite food, or dreaming of a holiday is a pleasurable experience. Going to the dentist or worrying about paying off the mortgage generally feels unpleasant. A neutral experience might be something like brushing your teeth.

We have fast-brain conditioned responses to each of these experiences. When we experience pleasant sensations, our automatic response is to want more, to cling to and become greedily attached to that experience. The conditioned response to unpleasant sensations is aversion and avoidance—we think, 'anything but this'. The conditioned response to neutral experiences is to numb out or go into autopilot. For example, when brushing your teeth, you're probably not particularly present. Most likely, your mind is wandering—you're zoned out. Mindfulness refers to this as a state of delusion.

When we get caught up in and are 'subject to' these reactions—clinging to the pleasant, aversion to the unpleasant or delusion in the neutral—we are less present and connected with life. We are reacting to life, rather than truly making our own choices. This results in less life satisfaction and more suffering. Understanding this second foundation of mindfulness is critical to exploring quadrant 4 of the matrix, in which we find our unconscious fears (aversion), attachments (clinging) and assumptions (delusion). In essence, these are the three core unconscious and conditioned drivers of our moving-away behaviours in quadrant 3 of the matrix.

With developmental mindfulness practices, such as those accompanying our programs, we begin to see the reactivity apart from the actual unpleasant, pleasant or neutral experience. This is a huge milestone on the self-awareness, vertical growth journey. It enables genuine self-regulation.

We develop the capacity to discern and differentiate our underlying conditioned, fast-brain reactions from what is objectively going on. This enables a vastly larger range of slow-brain prefrontal cortex choices. When we are receiving tough feedback, for example, we can notice the reactivity and tension in the body, and the defensive stories and aversive patterns at play. We can differentiate our aversive feelings from the reality of the feedback we are being given, lean into the discomfort and maintain curiosity, instead of being swept away in the aversive patterns to an unpleasant experience.

Understanding this second foundation has been absolutely life-changing for me. For example, when I experience any degree of suffering, I ask myself, *Michael, what are you in aversion to, and what are you attached to?*

I have discovered through years of practice that when I am attached to a goal or outcome, I am running away from, or in aversion to, some feeling inside myself. And when I am resisting an experience, like challenging feedback, I am unconsciously attached to a constructed identity of who I am or who I am not, and/or a good feeling inside myself. They are two sides of the same coin. I have come to understand that all unnecessary psychological suffering and dissatisfaction can be tracked back to either clinging or aversion, and only when we are free of these very deep conditioned patterns can awareness, satisfaction, unconditional love and happiness arise.

There is no escape from the pain of life, and no joy lasts forever. The attempt to escape pain or constantly grab at joy creates infinitely more suffering than we realise and all too often pushes us back into fast-brain reactivity.

Figure 7.1 presents a very simple summary of the second foundation of mindfulness.

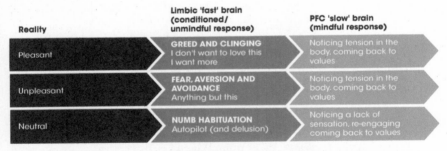

Figure 7.1: the second foundation of self-awareness

The third foundation of mindfulness: Thoughts

The first foundation of mindfulness is being aware of sensations we feel in our physical body; the second is noticing our reactivity to experiences. The third foundation is being mindful of our thoughts. We may not be able to feel our thoughts directly, but we can notice them and see them as object, rather than being unconsciously subject to them and their effects.

Often, however, our thoughts trigger physical and emotional sensations. For example, think of someone who has really hurt you, and focus on a particularly hurtful experience with this person. As you're sitting there thinking about that experience, do you notice any emotions arise? Do those emotions register physically? Do you feel any tension or heat in your body?

The more we can make our thoughts object to us, the less they control us. We can notice them without reacting to them or believing they are true.

For those with little mindfulness training, this foundation can be very challenging. Most people just don't have enough trained stability of awareness to be able to 'watch' thoughts without becoming involved and swept away by them. There are, however, many amazing mindfulness practices we can use to begin creating space in our awareness to observe thoughts and even learn what our thoughts are teaching us about our assumptions, obsessions and avoidances.

The fourth foundation of mindfulness: The way we make meaning

What we think and feel, our thoughts and emotions, are often the result of unseen, unquestioned assumptions we make about life. For example, suppose that as a result of my upbringing I have developed the unconscious assumption that everyone is judging me. Without even understanding it, I'll go through life being triggered by everyone I believe is judging me. I'll see judgement where it really doesn't exist.

The problem isn't that our assumptions are necessarily wrong; rather, it's that they are hidden and therefore control us without our conscious awareness.

Revathi Rammohan, CFO and Head of Research Operations for Novartis Institutes of Biomedical Research, shared with me how encountering different cultures around the world throughout her career has exposed her own cultural assumptions, and how this has helped her to become a better leader. She said, 'Earlier in my career corporate India was very hierarchical. You are taught in school just to listen to your teacher and don't ask questions. In a corporate setting, you never interrupt your boss or speak against him.

'Later, when I worked in the UK and the US, it was completely different. Here in the US, if you don't ask questions, you're not engaging, you're not learning. Because of my upbringing, I came into my position being very soft and deferential. I tend to be indirect rather than direct. I want to consider other people's feelings. I've had to challenge myself to become more direct. And I'm continually surprised by all the false assumptions I had, which I couldn't see until experiencing a different culture. For example, sometimes it's actually kinder to be more direct than indirect.'

There are three assumptions about life in particular that most of us are subject to.

False assumption #1: We can have a steady, fixed, constantly safe and pleasant destination in life.

The human mind is terrified of impermanence, so much of what we do in life, from the political and economic structures we create to the career path we choose, is motivated by the desire to create a sense of permanence and security. This is a delusion, because impermanence—constant change—is the very nature of reality. Reality is endlessly shifting and moving, and anything we hold onto—whether it's feelings or possessions—is always at risk of slipping away.

Suppose I really want a new car, because I think it will bring me happiness. I save for it and finally buy it. I'm thrilled. But when I go to the store and park it in the parking lot, I'm suddenly terrified that someone is going to scratch it. My peace of mind depends on this inanimate object staying just as it is.

This constant grasping for permanence is an endless source of discomfort and suffering. One of the primary goals of mindfulness is to help us be okay with the discomforts that inevitably pass through our lives. The good news is that they too are impermanent, and need to be accepted as such. Buddhist monk Pema Chodron suggests,

'Impermanence is a principle of harmony. When we don't struggle against it, we are in harmony with reality.'

False assumption #2: Resisting pain, especially emotional pain such as boredom, fear, sadness and hurt, leads to less pain and more peace in the long term.

Life will always have its traumas, challenges, losses and pain. Mindfulness is learning to accept these experiences without making them worse through resistance. As human development and addiction expert Gabor Maté puts it, 'The attempt to escape from pain is what creates more pain.'

Drug addiction, for example, is often experienced by people trying to escape the pain of a traumatic past. While drugs may give them temporary release, they cause long-term destruction. The only way out of the loop of addiction is to learn to be at peace with the thoughts and feelings one is trying to escape through the addictive substance or behaviour. It's also important to understand that addiction can be extremely subtle; for example, some people are addicted to control or to being right or even to certain thought loops. We all have our addictions.

False assumption #3: Numbing uncomfortable feelings through fast-brain addictive habits can lead to growth and a sustainably happy mind.

Numbing, or what mindfulness theory calls delusion, creates a gnawing sense of dissatisfaction. Ironically, the more we numb our uncomfortable feelings, the less we enjoy the feelings we really want in our life. In her book *The Gifts of Imperfection*, research professor Brené Brown explains, 'We cannot selectively numb emotion. If we numb the dark, we numb the light. If we take the edge off pain and discomfort, we are, by default, taking the edge off joy, love, belonging, and the other emotions that give meaning to our lives.'

The four foundations in practice

One day while meditating I noticed a lot of tension in my body (first foundation). I explored that tension and brought my awareness to the thoughts driving it (third foundation). I realised that the tension I was feeling was driven by thoughts about my to-do list. I was feeling stressed and anxious because I felt like I had too much to do.

My next inquiry was, *What am I clinging to and assuming that is creating these thoughts and this tension?* (second and fourth foundations). I realised I was clinging to the assumption that when I have completed my to-do list I'll have peace. But this is obviously untrue, since to-do lists are never-ending. To be alive is to have a to-do list.

After this inquiry, realising the false assumptions and thoughts creating the tension in my body, I was able to settle my mind and find peace in the present moment. The clinging eased, and my resistance to the anxiety in my body settled.

As another example, several years ago I was invited to do a training session for a client who had decided to run an offsite in the Australian vacation town of Noosa. My client paid for my flight from Sydney. I happened to have another client permanently based in Noosa whose internal policies precluded paying for flights. My thinking was that I could fly there on the flight provided by the first client, and then spend some time with the second client while I was there. It didn't occur to me at the time to tell the client who was paying for the flights that I was also going to work with another client who wasn't paying for the flights.

I lined up sessions with the first client who paid for my flight on Monday and Tuesday, and sessions with the other client on Wednesday and Thursday. On Tuesday morning my client asked, 'What time are you flying home tonight?'

I said, 'I'm not flying home tonight.'

'Oh, why?' asked the client.

In that moment I had a fast-brain response. I blatantly lied and said, 'I've got friends here in Noosa, so I'll stay the night and see them tomorrow.'

My CEO client responded, 'Oh, that's great. I hope you enjoy it.'

Ironically, that particular day I was facilitating a program on integrity-based leadership. As I was walking away to the parking garage, I noticed a physical reaction: I felt nauseous (first foundation). The body never lies, and it was telling me I had strayed from integrity.

That's when my mind kicked in with thoughts (third foundation) of how to handle the situation. My first thought was to tell the CEO the truth, to admit I had just lied to him and to apologise, which would probably result in my losing the client. Then I thought I could rationalise and tell a white lie to smooth things over. My mind even reasoned that it would be irresponsible of me to tell the truth, because I'm the sole breadwinner for my family and I would likely lose the client.

As all these thoughts raced through my head, I realised that the rationalising and excusing thoughts were about managing my discomfort—I was just trying to make my unpleasant feelings go away (second foundation). And it was clear that, in order for me to truly live my values, my only real choice was to come clean with the CEO.

This is the inescapable truth I have realised: we cannot outrun our own mind, and if we want a deeply happy mind, numbing and rationalising our misaligned behaviour is never going to get us what we want. Additionally, there is *never* going to be an easy, comfortable way to put this stuff into practice and vertically grow. If we wait for a risk-free, comfortable moment to develop our values and inner congruence, we will be waiting for the rest of our lives.

Even then, I didn't quite have the courage to overcome my embarrassment. So at first I didn't tell the CEO directly. Instead, I told the story to one of his direct reports, who reassured me: 'Oh, don't worry about it. We all do that. It's fine.'

My mind was still looking for a way to avoid the discomfort, so I thought, 'Great, I'm off the hook.' But my body was telling me otherwise.

Later that day I finally mustered up the courage to be completely honest with the CEO. He was surprised that I shared the story and was grateful. He even continued working with me.

Mindfulness and subject–object theory

As mentioned previously, in subject–object theory, *subject* refers to the things we can't see as separate from ourselves. They are fused with our identity, so we have no control over them.

For example, suppose I'm subject to the desire to impress others. Since I'm not conscious of that desire or the underlying causes of it, I can't change it. It will continually show up in my behaviour—for example, when I take credit for ideas that aren't mine, claim that my ideas are always best, brag about my accomplishments or try to win at everything, even casual board games.

The only way for me to overcome this behaviour is to make it object to me, which means seeing it objectively, rather than as an unquestioned part of my self-identity. When it becomes object to me, I have the psychological flexibility to transform my behaviour. I can give others credit for their ideas and edify others instead of bragging about myself.

In the simplest terms, to be mindful of something is to make it object. The only things we are not mindful of within ourselves are the things to which we are subject. If I say, 'Be mindful of your need to impress when you chat with your team today,' I mean, don't become subject to that need and all its associated patterns of thinking and behaving. And if you are mindful of it, then in those moments you will not be subject to or ruled by the need to impress. It's that direct relationship between subject–object theory and developmental mindfulness.

Mindfulness gives us the ability to see the things we've been subject to our whole lives. Mindfulness, in fact, delivers an amazingly clear process for making subject into object over the long term. The first intent of mindfulness is to reduce psychological suffering and its associated fast-brain thinking and behaving. It is only possible to continue with these thoughts and behaviours if we are subject to them, and therefore unknowingly invested in them.

The first clue mindfulness gives us is the development of a sensitivity to what is really going on inside us. The second clue is noticing suffering in the body and mind. As soon as we notice tension in the body, resistance to our feelings, or desperate repeated ruminating and thinking, we can be sure we are subject to and fused with something that is not helpful to us. This is where a developmental mindfulness skillset becomes your greatest ally in your vertical growth journey. It enables you to systematically make all that you are subject to into object. This is the fastest route to the end of all unnecessary internal suffering.

It then supports our capacity to operate from the slow brain, so we author the kind of actions that reduce our suffering and that of others. We can cultivate the deepest levels of psychological safety within and without. Without mindfulness, the adult development process is extremely slow. Mindfulness is like turbo-boosting the growth process.

As James Skinner at EY explained it, 'Mindfulness gives me the ability to step back and observe my thoughts, feelings and assumptions. Then I can actually use those observations to shape how I act and behave going forward, rather than being subject to them. I can more consciously choose how to behave in order to get the outcome I want, or the impact on others.'

8
Overcome numbness and denial

'It is the person who continues in his self-deception and ignorance who is harmed.'
Marcus Aurelius

W e've now explored the centre of the Mindful Leader Matrix, self-awareness and self-regulation, and the operating system that moves us either towards or away from our values. Now let's dive deeper into the left side of the matrix to better understand the dynamics that move us away from our values. This is where we begin to systematically 'make object' the fears, attachments, assumptions and behaviours that move us away from our aspirations, or the talk we are trying to walk as leaders.

Carl Jung, one of the fathers of modern western psychology, spoke of the 'shadow' in relation to our capacity to hide from ourselves and deny our own behaviours, thoughts, feelings and beliefs. We keep them in the shadow of our mind through defence mechanisms such as numbing, denying, blaming and justifying, instead of bringing them into the light of our awareness. Yet literally everything we are subject to is held in the unconscious, which is why Jung was so insistent that we work on the shadow element of our unconscious in order to grow and rediscover wholeness. In adult development language, we would say that until we make our shadow object to us, we will continue to be subject to it. In other words, vertical growth depends on our willingness and ability to look at and work with our shadow. The shadow is what we explore on the left side of the matrix.

In chapter 6 we differentiated between developmental and calming mindfulness practices. Developmental mindfulness practices are a very important skillset for the navigation and resolution of our shadow. Calming mindfulness practices, however, can keep us perpetually in denial of our shadow, which is why they don't tend to support real vertical growth.

To see our shadow, we must first overcome numbness and denial

Being accountable for our behaviour requires self-awareness and clarity. Before we can change a behaviour, we first have to see it clearly and understand where it's coming from. We must recognise our shadow side, which creates unconscious behaviours that move us away from a values-based and self-examined life.

The human mind has many mechanisms to prevent us from feeling the pain of facing our shadow. Our ego structure will function to maintain its current state, the identity that has served to protect us over the years, but this protection also creates our prison, as it limits our ability to grow and explore new possibilities. It keeps us in a safe box rather than unlocking our hidden potential and a more expansive version or ourselves.

To the untrained mind, the solution to dealing with stress and pain is found in either pleasure or denial and numbness. Whenever we encounter unpleasant feelings, our mind immediately looks for ways to alleviate them. Instead of looking inward, we drown out the unpleasantness by indulging in food, alcohol, sex, binge TV or social media—anything to escape the pain.

Numbness fogs our brain. It conceals our shadow and helps us avoid the pain of facing it, but it also eclipses the sun of connection and joy. Numbness reduces the pain, but it also reduces our happiness and fulfilment.

In our work we refer to numbness and denial as the 'first line of defence'. The mind has an extraordinary ability to embrace denial of what we are doing. We snap, 'I am not angry!' If we're able to break through this first line of defence using mindfulness, and to acknowledge our unconscious behaviour and the painful feelings associated with that admission, a 'second line of defence' usually kicks in: justification, rationalisation or blame. These devices are designed once again to numb us, masking the shadow. We discuss this more in the next chapter.

Numbness is a fast-brain activity we engage in for short-term pain relief. It may be appealing in the short term, but it is fundamentally unsatisfying. It robs us of connection and joy, and it ensures that we keep acting against our deepest aspirations without even realising it. The challenge with numbness is that we can't see it, precisely because we are numb. It's like living a half-life—everything is a bit dull and lifeless, but at least it's not so painful.

Other coping mechanisms can also express themselves, such as the fight, flight or freeze response (see table 8.1).

Table 8.1: common fight, flight or freeze behaviours

Fight	Flight	Freeze
becoming argumentative	withdrawing (physically or mentally)	not speaking up
blaming	avoiding people or conversations	downplaying self-worth
raising voice and tone competitiveness	procrastinating tasks becoming demotivated	isolating oneself conforming to group norms
supporting rumours		

In all of these protective behaviours, the invitation is to bring awareness to them and cultivate compassion for them, understanding that their purpose is to protect you. While being aware of these protective behaviours, instead of lost in them, you can then consciously choose to move towards the behaviours most aligned with your values and aspirations.

How the inner judge triggers numbness

On the surface, numbness makes no rational sense, as it very clearly derails our best intentions. So why do we do it?

One of the primary reasons is that we're ashamed of behaviours that violate our values. We don't want to be the person who values health and wellbeing but eats junk food, or who values honesty but often lies. So instead of facing our shame head-on with curiosity, we sweep it under the rug through numbness.

Looking deeper, where does our sense of shame come from, the shame we avoid through unconscious, fast-brain numbness? It comes from our harsh inner judge.

Do you remember the last time you made a big mistake? How did you feel? What did your inner conversation sound like? What kinds of things did you tell yourself? Let me guess: You felt ashamed or embarrassed. You beat yourself up and called yourself names, like 'stupid'. You vowed never to make that mistake again. Does this sound familiar?

Of course, every human being on the planet can relate to it. We all have this inner judge. We all criticise and reproach ourselves. We all struggle with self-esteem at times. It's like we have two people inside us, and however hard we try, we can never seem to win an argument with our inner judge. The judge overpowers any countervailing thoughts or arguments.

But the inner judge is far more than just a voice in our head. That voice creates an actual physical experience. It can trigger fear and shame, which feel tight and hot in the body. It's an unpleasant sensation that we long to shake off. When active, it can inflict a tremendous amount of suffering on the body.

For example, suppose I value healthy eating. One day, feeling stress from work, I find myself eating a lot of junk food. My inner judge kicks in, 'Michael, you're weak and pathetic. You say you want to be healthy, but you can't resist junk food.' That feeling of shame creates intense distress and pain, which paradoxically leads to a vicious cycle of yet more short-term relief behaviours, which increases the likelihood that we will continually escape into them.

Where does the inner judge come from?

Imagine you're a four-year-old child. Every day you take a walk with your mother. Whenever you come to an intersection, she holds your hand and says, 'Make sure you always look both ways before crossing the street.'

Sometimes you forget to look both ways. Just as you start to cross, your mother yells at you to stop then scolds you, 'How many times do I have to tell you? You *must* look both ways before you cross the street!' You feel ashamed under her scolding.

One time you're crossing the street alone, and your mother's voice comes into your mind: 'Look both ways before you cross.' Not wanting to feel the shame of disobedience, you follow her rule, look both ways then quickly cross the street.

This simple example illustrates how the inner judge is formed. When we're little, and our brain is at its most plastic, our parents and other adults teach us rules for survival. In our young minds, they are golden rules that offer us safety, love and guidance, and teach us about the world out there. At some point, we internalise this authoritative advice so it becomes the voice of our inner judge.

The rules imposed on us as children do help us to survive, but it comes at a cost. The voices of our parents, teachers and other influencers weren't always kind. We often received the message that we were doing things wrong, that we were stupid, that we weren't measuring up to expectations, that we were just not good enough. We were constantly hectored with 'shoulds' and 'musts'.

For adults, the inner judge is fundamentally an obsolete system rooted in a lack of trust. It comprises the voices of correction, blame, shame, criticism and humiliation we were assaulted with as children. While it kept us safe, now, as adults, it stifles our potential and kills inner psychological safety.

The purpose of the inner judge

The tactics the inner judge uses against us are self-destructive, but strangely they have the best of intentions. If we bring our curiosity to our inner judge, it feels like the voice of a parent or carer, someone who has our back, a guide who constantly seeks to steer us in the right direction, to align with its ideas of right and wrong. It helps us to grow, to be safe and to learn. Its core message is, 'If you listen to me, you'll be loved and you'll be secure.'

The problem with the inner judge is that, while it seeks to guide us and teach us, it is completely devoid of curiosity, which is at the heart of all growth and learning. It doesn't explain *why* it wants us to behave in a certain way; it only demands that we obey, and when we don't it tends to get stronger and stronger. It's like it's a combination of inner parent, teacher and bully.

Not only is our inner judge devoid of curiosity, but it is also unkind. It will say anything to get us to comply. It shames and criticises and beats us down, desperate to get us to avoid the shame of making mistakes. And in the process, it holds us hostage to its rules and expectations. Our inner judge is the root cause of all our insecurities and lack of growth, and until we can understand it, we cannot transcend it.

Self-compassion creates inner psychological safety

Our inner judge has often been conditioned early in life as our parents, teachers and other significant authority figures in our life corrected or punished us, at times with good intentions and at times as a consequence of their own trauma and shadow. These external influences often generate a belief that, *if I'm not self-critical and tough on myself, I will not grow and improve.* Unfortunately, this strategy is often short-lived and further activates our fast brain, reinforcing our destructive patterns and moving-away behaviours.

In order to grow, we have to recognise our avoidant behaviours and deal with them. This requires us to neutralise our inner judge.

Along with curiosity, the best way to neutralise the inner judge is through self-compassion. As I like to put it, *truth and compassion are blood brothers.* Curiosity brings us to truth, and truth can be confronting. When we view some truth inside ourselves with judgement, facing truth becomes an emotionally unsafe process. Self-compassion calms the fast brain, opening up neural pathways to the slow brain and creating a world of new options and opportunities rather than remaining stuck in past algorithms.

We can only see and deal with truth if it is emotionally safe to do so. This safety depends on self-compassion and access to our slower brain. Self-compassion is holding ourselves in a warm and open-hearted embrace, feeling our suffering, grieving for it and supporting ourselves in it. Self-compassion is a voice of deep care and concern, non-judgemental and kind.

Sheila Frame, at Amryt Pharma, captured the essence of self-compassion elegantly when she told me, 'I really wish I could help people understand that they are enough. That's the real beauty of inner work—to realise that you are enough. We don't have to rationalise or defend. We can be comfortable with and accept ourselves. And when we mess up, we can always own it and begin again.'

Being truly honest with ourselves isn't about seeing our 'badness' and punishing ourselves for it; rather, it's about seeing our basic goodness and forgiving ourselves for our ignorance and our conditioned reactions. We are far more motivated to be and do good by self-compassion than by shame and self-criticism. Author and trauma expert Gabor Maté writes, 'Only in the presence of compassion will people allow themselves to see the truth.' Margaret Dean, at Novartis, pointed out the obvious: 'We're self-harming all the time. I've realised that if I really believe in compassion and connection, then I have to start with myself and be self-compassionate.'

Revathi Rammohan, at Novartis, shared how difficult her mindfulness process has been, and how important self-compassion has been important in that process. 'Earlier in my career,' she said, 'I was a micromanager and I would often be controlling. I couldn't see how my controlling behaviour was violating my value of helping others grow and realise their potential. I thought I was helping them, but I was actually holding them back by not empowering them.

'It was easy to numb myself to this truth by telling myself stories of why I was right. I didn't want to look beneath the surface to see what was really happening.

'Through mindfulness training, I began to see my patterns. When you realise the impact you've had on people and the stress you've inflicted on them, it's not fun and it's not liberating. It's very disappointing. Instead of feeling lighter with my realisations, I felt heavy with remorse.

'To deal with this regret, I also had to learn how to forgive myself and to stop judging myself so harshly. That's when the real liberation came, when I realised that I didn't have to keep beating myself up. I could change and I could grow through self-compassion, not self-judgement.'

Steven Baert also told me, 'There needs to be a loving side of self-awareness. Otherwise, it can become judgement, which then becomes self-punishment. And once we start punishing ourselves, we start moving away from self-awareness, because why do we want to do that to ourselves? If self-awareness just leads to guilt and self-judgement, we won't do it. We have to be honest with ourselves. But to do that, we have to love and care for ourselves as well.'

Many research studies have shown that, in contrast with self-critical people, self-compassionate people:

- feel greater motivation to make amends and avoid repeating moral transgressions

- are more motivated to improve personal weaknesses

- are more likely to take responsibility for their past mistakes

- are more likely to set new goals for themselves after failing to meet previous goals.

Researcher Kristin Neff observes, 'Self-compassion is not the same as being easy on ourselves. It's a way of nurturing ourselves so that we can reach our full potential.' Mindfulness teacher Tara Brach points out in her book *Radical Acceptance*, 'Feeling compassion for ourselves in no way releases us from responsibility for our actions. Rather, it releases us from the self-hatred that prevents us from responding to our life with clarity and balance.'

Use the matrix to break the pattern of numbness

Our mind's tendency to cling to pleasant sensations and avoid unpleasant sensations, combined with our inner judge, creates a vicious, self-defeating cycle.

Here's how it works: we experience something unpleasant, which triggers a fast-brain numbing response designed to alleviate the associated difficult feelings. Then our inner judge kicks in and berates us for being 'bad', 'weak' or 'stupid'. In response to this harsh self-judgement, we kick into denial and rationalisation mode while the difficult feelings (the sense of guilt and shame) inevitably propel us back into numbing behaviours.

Suppose, for example, a manager holds the value of honesty. His team misses a project deadline, and his boss calls him in to ask why. He freezes in the moment. Reluctant to feel the shame of admitting his failures, his fast brain kicks in and he lies blatantly. Now his inner judge engages and begins berating him for being a liar, which triggers even more shame. So now he thinks of justifications: 'It was my team's fault.' 'My manager has unreal expectations.'

Finally, to soothe all these uncomfortable feelings, he engages in more numbing behaviours: having overeaten, he vegges out in front of the TV for hours.

As with all behavioural change, to break this pattern of numbness, we can use the Mindful Leader Matrix (see figure 8.1). For the manager in the example, his fear of being seen as incompetent, his attachment to his image and his assumption that leaders need to know everything (quadrant 4) triggered his unconscious, fast-brain response of lying (quadrant 3), which violated his core value of honesty (quadrant 1). His goal is to make the unconscious conscious, understand why he lied, work with his fears and attachments, question his assumptions and change his behaviour to align with his value of honesty (quadrant 2).

The first ingredient we need in this process is non-judgemental curiosity. As already noted, our inner judge is devoid of curiosity and prone to criticism, which raise unassailable barriers to vertical growth. It cannot see the deeper reasons behind the behaviours it shames us for.

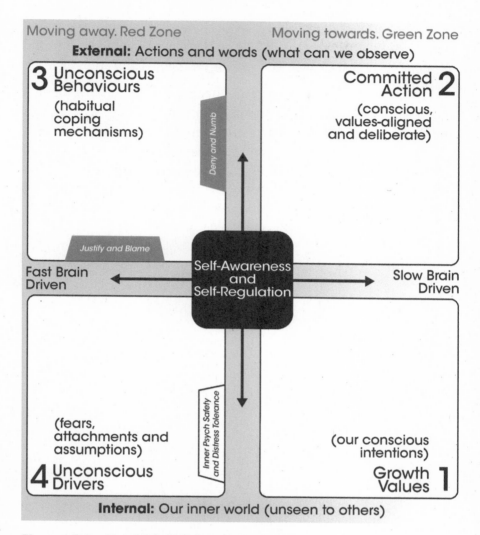

Figure 8.1: the Mindful Leader Matrix

By shifting from self-judgement to curiosity, the manager can explore why he lied in the moment. What was really behind that? What was he afraid of? These questions bring insight and awareness, which then enables vertical growth.

The next ingredient needed to break the cycle of numbness is self-compassion. An essential ally when seeking to achieve vertical growth is being kind to ourselves. When we engage in fast-brain activities and self-defeating behaviours, it's not because we're bad people. We're just human and, like all humans, we act from fear and blind habit and we struggle to feel safe, connected and appreciated.

With curiosity, we uncover our unconscious fears, attachments and assumptions. With self-compassion, we help ourselves accept and bear the fear and pain that arise when we see and own the truth of what is driving our dysfunctional behaviour. Our greater emotional regulation allows the slow brain to see and regulate the fast brain. Now we are prepared to get clear on what's really important to us, and to create an action plan for aligning our behaviour with our values.

9
See and resolve the shadow

'It is only through shadows that one comes to know the light.'
St. Catherine of Siena

arl Jung famously said, 'Until you make the unconscious conscious, it will direct your life and you will call it fate.' Mindfulness, supported by the Mindful Leader Matrix, is how we 'make the unconscious conscious'.

The impact our unconscious programming has on our behaviour cannot be overestimated. According to Harvard professor Gerald Zaltman, 95 per cent of our thoughts, emotions and learning occur without our conscious awareness. Most cognitive neuroscientists concur. NeuroFocus founder A. K. Pradeep goes even further and puts the figure at 99.999 per cent. Our subconscious thoughts and assumptions are like algorithms, programmed by our past traumas, reinforcements, punishments and cultural influences. Without the deep work linked to mindfulness and shadow work, this programming will continue to shape our lives, holding us back from the growth we are trying to cultivate.

Dan Ariely, professor of psychology and behavioural economics at Duke University and author of *Predictably Irrational: The Hidden Forces That Shape Our Decisions*, concludes from years of empirical research that 'we are pawns in a game whose forces we largely fail to comprehend'. David Eagleman, a neuroscientist at Baylor College of Medicine and author of *Incognito: The Secret Lives of the Brain*, writes, '[C]onsciousness is the smallest player in the operations of the brain. Our brains run mostly on autopilot, and the conscious mind has little access to the giant and mysterious factory that runs below it.'

Dealing with the bottom left the matrix can require literally a lifetime of inner development work. The first step is to address the shadow that is holding us back from living our growth values. The challenge is to uncover our unconscious assumptions and beliefs so we can have greater agency over them.

Uncovering the shadow

During a course I was teaching, a participant told me, 'I hate prejudiced people.'

'That's interesting,' I said. 'Do you see the issue with that statement?'

'No,' she replied.

'Prejudiced people often engage in hatred of others,' I explained. 'And you're engaging in the same. You are hating the haters. The result is that your opportunity to influence prejudiced people is greatly diminished.'

This is a simple illustration of how unconscious we can be as human beings. Not intentionally, and not because we're bad in any way, but simply because we're blind to what we're doing. We are blind to our shadow.

As previously noted, the shadow represents the parts of ourselves that we disown and repress because we are subconsciously afraid to admit the parts of ourselves that we find inferior or unacceptable. Psychologist Stephen Diamond explains that our shadow is dark 'both because it tends to consist predominantly of the primitive, negative, socially or religiously depreciated human emotions and impulses like sexual lust, power strivings, selfishness, greed, envy, anger, fear or rage, and due to its unenlightened nature, completely obscured from consciousness'.

Our shadow explains why we often behave in ways that are contrary to our values, while being in denial about it. As Carl Jung said, 'Everyone carries a shadow, and the less it is embodied in the individual's conscious life, the blacker and denser it is. At all counts, it forms an unconscious snag, thwarting our most well-meant intentions.'

Our shadow is the brain's way of protecting an identity that served us at one point in our lives. For example, Carl (Lemieux) had a client who received a lot of reinforcement for perfect grades when she was young. If she went home with a 95 per cent score for her exam, her father would ask what she had missed that prevented her from getting 100 per cent. She was sent the well-intended message, 'If you do something, do it well.' Unfortunately, she internalised the idea that perfection was necessary to get validation and love.

This unconscious conditioning led her to seek out perfection in every aspect of her life. In meetings she would always seek out what went wrong and identify missing details, which led to disengagement from her team and colleagues. She was very hard on herself too, always seeking out additional data points to validate her decisions, postponing decisions to ensure everything was perfect, revisiting the past and anticipating the future to reinforce her ego's unconscious drive for perfection, and hence self-preservation.

Recent research suggests that such conditioned responses protect our ego structure through our brain's default mode network (DMN). This neurological structure is responsible not only for protecting our physical wellbeing by scanning the environment and sending information to our limbic system (fast brain), but also for protecting our emotional wellbeing. This automatic reaction seeks not expansion or innovation, but protection.

As leaders, when not self-aware, we are thus driven by what appears to be the right thing to do based on what once served us well.

Without self-awareness, we are therefore not in a position to see objectively if our behaviours are adapted to the context, or whether they are a relic of our past that no longer serves us. In short, our shadow is the source of all our self-sabotaging behaviours. And the less we see it, the greater its destructive influence on our lives.

Ironically, others tend to see our shadow more easily than we do. When we're operating out of our shadow, it's often for grand display, and the only person being fooled is us. In our leadership development programs we help leaders to come clean with their team by openly discussing the shadow they have been leading from and asking their team to help them with compassionate feedback when it's happening, so they can recover credibility, trust and psychological safety. It's no surprise that leader after leader has told us that these sessions were completely life-changing for them. They were tough, but the most important development moments of their career.

Leaders do need to watch out for defence mechanisms when they start admitting to their shadow, however. They have achieved a vertical growth milestone by breaking down the first line of defence (numbness and denial) by admitting to and identifying their quadrant 3 behaviours of moving away from their values. But the second line of defence (justification and blame) can still easily kick in here, so they never reach the deeper understanding and growth available in quadrant 4.

To mitigate the intensity of the emotional pain of admitting the shadow, leaders can all too quickly revert to fast-brain protective habits like justification and blame. It might be, for example, 'I know I micromanage, but I just love attention to detail,' or, 'I just insist on excellence.' We always have a good story to explain our darker side. Of course, we also don't ever reach the fourth quadrant of shadow exploration if we flip into self-criticism and blame ourselves. Inner psychological safety disappears, and with it the curiosity and compassion needed for exploring quadrant 4.

This kind of growth work is not easy, which is why the more advanced stages of vertical growth are rare and remarkable. As Jung taught, 'One does not become enlightened by imagining figures of light, but by making the darkness conscious. The latter procedure, however, is disagreeable and therefore not popular.'

Interestingly, Jung wasn't interested in organisational development or team and leadership performance. He was interested in personal and transpersonal psychology, the process of helping people find happiness and wellbeing. He studied the shadow because it plays an integral role in our mental health. It runs on autopilot beneath the surface of what we think are conscious choices, constantly eroding our health and wellbeing and causing incongruence and stress in our lives. When we're not conscious of it, it creates constant internal conflict. We're in denial of some of our urges and behaviours. For our happiness alone, dealing with the shadow is a good idea.

Initially, when we begin exploring and owning our shadow, it can be extremely painful. However, exposing and understanding our whole selves, warts and all, is the best long-term path to happiness and fulfilment. It enables a profoundly mature and relaxed mind, free of defence and denial. Those who have done deep shadow work have also done deep compassion work. They are indivisible.

In today's turbulent organisational context where human suffering is on the rise, the deeper practices found in clinical psychology are increasingly needed to help people discover the psychological wellbeing to support healthy organisational performance.

Using the Mindful Leader Matrix to see and resolve the shadow in quadrants 3 and 4

The Mindful Leader Matrix gives us a framework for exploring our shadow mindfully and resolving it so we can more easily live up to our aspirations (see figure 9.1, overleaf).

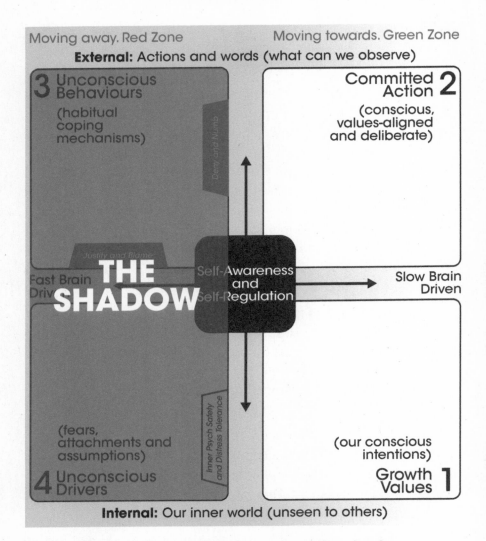

Figure 9.1: using the matrix to explore the shadow

Margaret Dean, at Novartis, opened up with me about how her shadow has played out in her leadership. She has always had a very strong achievement drive. While this drive has served her well in many regards, it has also given her blind spots and created less-than-ideal leadership behaviours (quadrant 3). For example, she would set very high expectations for herself then beat herself up when she didn't achieve them. Her default mode was, in her words, 'to work hard, move fast, and get stuff done and delivered'. This meant that she would often not stop to reflect or ensure team involvement.

Her belief was that working hard and moving fast served her short-term needs to feel useful and gain recognition for getting things done. These reactive behaviours were feeding her more primitive brain and socialised mind, rather than allowing her to work from a self-examined mind adapted to her current environment.

During a vertical growth exercise in which she was uncovering these patterns, she asked herself, *Why did I become so attached to using achievement as a mechanism to demonstrate my value?* Her answer was, 'When I was a child, my family moved around a lot. I was constantly being put into environments where I was the outsider, and I knew that if I wanted to be accepted and to belong, I had to perform and achieve.' The quadrant 4 attachment and assumption were driving her quadrant 3 behaviours.

To transform her quadrant 3 behaviours, Margaret first had to become more conscious about what was important to her. She recounted, 'I started challenging the assumption that life is about achieving. Is that really what I want my life to be about? I concluded that achievement is important if it's in the service of making a difference, having impact and making the world a better place. But if it shuts down connection with people, which is equally, if not more, important to me than achievement, then it's not worth it. 'I'm often moving so fast or so focused on the task at hand that I miss signals from people. My unconscious attachment to speed means I'm not seeing that people aren't buying into what we're doing, or they may be burned out.'

Through this process, Margaret was shocked to see how much of a blind spot she had in this regard. 'I had told my team that I wanted to create a place where people can really be their authentic selves and bring their gifts to the world. And I want to really connect and create a community where we all feel that we don't have to self-protect and we can be ourselves.

'I was crushed when I received 360° feedback from my team and they told me that I don't create space for that. It was a crushing blow to think that what you're aspiring to do isn't happening because this pattern is constantly getting in your way.'

So to counteract the limiting fears, attachments and assumptions in her quadrant 4, Margaret consciously chose the value of connection in quadrant 1. But in order to fully transform, she then needed to attach a specific behaviour in quadrant 2 to support her value of connection. She chose the practice of listening. She said, 'The practice of listening helps me to rein in my achievement drive and slow everything down. I invite more perspectives, more curiosity, more challenging of assumptions. And more than anything, I can create that safe space for people to connect.'

Steven Baert described how from a young age he has always been clear on two of his core values: responsibility and care for others. While you might say that these values are in quadrant 1, in fact Steven had some unconscious patterns in his shadow that made him misapply these values.

He explained, 'Because I've always been the one who was responsible and caring for others, leadership responsibility has often been assigned to me without me seeking it out. Even when I was a child, parents would feel comfortable sending their sons out with me because they knew they could trust me to be responsible.

'As a result, I've always taken up more responsibility than I initially asked for. And that comes with pride, but it's also exhausting. Because I do care about and feel responsible for those around me, and I suffer when things don't go the way I had envisioned for them. So there's a beautiful side to that responsibility, but there's also an element that eats at me and very quickly depletes my energy.'

When I asked Steven to list specific quadrant 3 behaviours that resulted from his unconscious patterns, he responded, 'I would sandwich and sugarcoat feedback. Or I would procrastinate and avoid it altogether. I would go into a meeting telling everyone I was going to share feedback, then I would postpone it until the end and be happy if we ran out of time. But on top of that, after avoiding tough conversations, I would get irritated and flip to the opposite end of the scale and eventually give feedback from an irritated fast-brain place in myself.'

Ironically, because of his unconscious assumptions, attachments and fears in quadrant 4, his values of responsibility and care were actually conflicting with each other. As he put it, 'The story I told myself was that I couldn't both hold people accountable and expect them to deliver on something, while at the time being caring and loving. I felt that at some point I had to make a choice between these values. So I would initially choose care and love, hoping that the person would deliver without me needing to push them. And when they didn't deliver, suddenly my sense of responsibility would be so high that I could no longer take it and I would flip from a very caring and loving person to, "Enough, it's time to make a change." This eroded trust in my team because people couldn't understand how I could flip that switch from a nice, caring guy who behaves like a friend to a pushy boss.'

To uncover Steven's quadrant 4 fears, attachments and assumptions, I asked him what was beneath these behaviours. 'I often doubted my own judgement and I craved the loyalty of my team members,' he revealed. 'I needed their loyalty to get the task done. And I was worried that giving them feedback would damage the relationship. So I prioritised relationships over tasks, but I rewarded tasks over relationships. And that's where the tension was.'

'What assumption created that dissonance in your values?' I asked.

'The illusion was that if I really invest in a strong relationship and win their loyalty, they will deliver on the work I need them to do. And if I give them honest feedback, I will hurt their feelings, the relationship will suffer, and as a result the task will break down.'

This was the consciousness Steven needed to balance his values of responsibility and care and break his quadrant 3 behaviours. He explained, 'The beauty of this process was then, when I saw my patterns, I realised that there was no tension between my values. In fact, when applied consciously, they are complementary and mutually supporting. When I see someone who is not delivering and needs to be held accountable, and I don't have that conversation, that shows a lack of loving and caring. The caring thing to do is to have that direct conversation. That's how people grow. Whereas if I don't have that conversation, I am actually betraying both of my values of responsibility and care.'

The fruition of this process is that Steven chose as his quadrant 1 practice to give people regular, constructive feedback. As a result, his values are no longer in conflict and he has cultivated more trust with his team members and a much happier, more congruent inner world.

One reason why shadow work is so important is that it can even distort the application of the finest virtues or values. The mindfulness literature sometimes refers to this as the 'near enemy' of our virtues. It's so close to the real thing that it's very easy to miss that it's based on fear or anger.

Jenelle McMaster, Deputy CEO and Markets Leader at professional services organisation EY Oceania, discovered this. Throughout her career, Jenelle has always been clear on her core values: humility, respect and positivity. What she hasn't been clear on, however, is how she has often lived from the shadow side of those values.

'I always thought my humility was an asset,' she told me. 'But I've learned how my unconsciousness around it has severely limited my career. For example, I've suffered from "imposter syndrome" my whole life. This fear that I don't belong has often made me play small. But I've often hidden behind that fear in the name of humility. It's almost like I can use my imposter syndrome as a badge of honour—as in, look at me humbly going about my business, not seeking the spotlight, not putting myself above others.

'However, what I've realised is that playing small isn't about humility at all. In fact, ironically, it's about image management, being attached to looking humble to others, which is the opposite of humility. Instead of my humility being about serving others, its shadow side is that it's really just my fear of standing out and being exposed as not smart enough for my position.'

In Jenelle's quadrant 4, we find her attachment to *looking* humble and her fear and assumption that she isn't good enough. This subconscious quadrant 4 fear, attachment and assumption has created a lot of unconscious quadrant 3 behaviour. For example, when she did not understand things in meetings she wouldn't ask certain clarifying questions for fear of exposing her gaps in understanding.

For Jenelle to grow past this pattern of false humility, she had to get clear on what was most important to her. In this case, she chose the value of curiosity. She explained, 'Curiosity is spurred by the desire to keep growing, and that's what I want to do. I feel like I'm holding myself back from growth through a lack of curiosity. And the lack of curiosity comes from fear. I don't want to be exposed for how little I know, so I pull back and hide. With curiosity, I'm less concerned about how I look to others and more concerned about learning and growing.'

So after consciously choosing the value of curiosity in her quadrant 1, Jenelle's next step was to attach specific behaviours to that value. In her words, this boiled down to, 'You will now see me asking more questions and saying yes to more things that I would have said no to in the past out of fear.'

As a result, Jenelle has become far more aware of the shadow side of her values and is consciously choosing a better way. Now her value of humility genuinely serves her, rather than limiting her.

Nathalie Bouchard, General Manager of the Ubisoft Quebec studio, a large international video game development company, had a similar experience. One of her core values is responsibility, which is obviously a very healthy value to cultivate. However, a shadow side to that responsibility hindered her leadership.

She explained, 'I want things to get done the right way so badly that I can be a control freak. I try to control my environment. I'm results-driven and I can be a little intense.'

'And how would that show up in your actual behaviour?' I asked.

'I stop listening,' she said. 'Even if I ask you a question, I will hear you, but I won't listen, because I'm already working on a solution instead of letting the other person find answers and solutions for themselves.'

'So,' I asked, 'would it be fair to say that in those moments, your value of responsibility is being violated because you're not allowing people to come to their own responsibility?'

'Exactly,' she agreed. 'I take responsibility for others, which is control, not responsibility at all.'

'And where does your attachment to control come from?' I pressed.

She said, 'I fear failing. I fear not doing the right thing. I fear not being loved or not being appreciated. So I feel like I have to know the answers or I will fail or not be valued.'

Like Jenelle, the insight Nathalie gained in exploring her shadow in quadrant 4 helped her understand how she was distorting her value of responsibility in support of her need to control others. This enabled a far wiser application of her quadrant 2 commitment.

Discover your unconscious assumptions

What causes stress in your life?

We've asked this question of leaders and teams for over 20 years. The vast majority of responses fall into one of three categories: other people (such as my colleagues or my spouse), external circumstances (such as a lack of job security or money, uncertainty about the future or heavy commuter traffic), structures and systems (such as too many meetings or bosses or demands, or an excessive workload). The common theme across all these responses is the belief that ongoing stress is solely caused by *external factors*.

Our proposition, however, is that with the exception of genuinely life-threatening circumstances, our ongoing stress is internally generated and both largely unseen and mismanaged. In other words, it's not caused by these external things; it's actually caused by our internal expectations and assumptions, our mindset and our unconscious conditioning.

Although our brains are more evolved than those of other animals, under stress we are at a significant disadvantage. In his classic book on stress, *Why Zebras Don't Get Ulcers*, researcher Robert Sapolsky explains why. When attacked by a lion—a much more stressful situation than we humans typically face—a zebra will launch into flight mode. Triggered by its sympathetic nervous system, its body is flooded with fear-based chemicals to mobilise its effort to escape. But when the zebra has escaped and the threat is over, within minutes it will go right back to eating in a relaxed state, responding to the parasympathetic nervous system, also known as the 'rest and digest' system.

It's a very different story for humans because of our mind's tendency towards negative rumination, meaning we repetitively return to our negative emotional experience to rehash its causes, situational factors, solutions and consequences. In short, we replay both past and future, imagined stressful situations over and over in our mind, thus exacerbating our stress and undermining our mental wellbeing. Almost all of this obsessive rumination is based on a false assumption—that stress is always caused by and therefore always resolved by a change in external factors, rather than a change in mindset.

If you believe that all stress is caused by external factors, consider the example of two people stuck in traffic on their way to work, both of whom will be late unless traffic conditions ease. One is calm and relaxed, knowing that getting stressed or angry won't make the traffic go faster or help the situation in any way. The second is frustrated, angry and stressed, leaning on her horn and cursing other drivers.

The second driver unconsciously assumes that the traffic is the cause of her stress, but if external factors were the sole cause of the stress, they would create stress for everyone equally. Yet in this example and countless others, this clearly is not the case. While the external world gives us plenty of triggers and challenges, and can be thoroughly unpleasant, the ultimate cause of our ongoing stress is the way we process our experience internally.

Find the fears, attachments and assumptions causing your stress

Let's look at this stress example in the context of the Mindful Leader Matrix. The stressed driver might begin to shout, grit her teeth, ruminate and panic, all behaviours that sit in quadrant 3. This behaviour is an attempt to reduce the short-term discomfort of being stuck in traffic (lack of mindfulness). This behaviour unfortunately works against her core values of calmness and respect, which is the realm of quadrant 1 (see figure 9.2).

To remember to consistently cultivate calmness instead (quadrant 2), it is very helpful to identify her unconscious fears, attachments and assumptions (quadrant 4) driving the unconscious behaviour in quadrant 3. These might include 'It's impossible to be calm in traffic', or 'I'm just so attached to the idea that there should be no traffic on the roads', or 'If I could just live in a city with no traffic, then I would happy.'

To help people uncover their unconscious fears, attachments and assumptions in quadrant 4 in an organisational context, typically we don't explore deep childhood conditioning and trauma. This is the realm of deeper therapy work, and it's not psychologically safe to explore these aspects in the workplace. Instead, we borrow from Kegan and Lahey's work on immunity to change, and our second foundation of mindfulness work on clinging, aversion and delusion, and we use the following four questions:

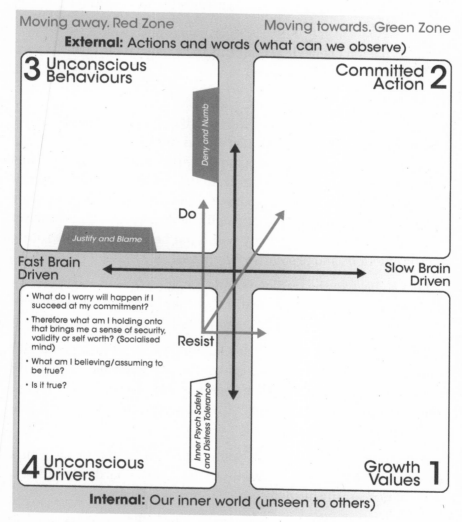

Figure 9.2: why we engage in quadrant 3 behaviours and resist quadrants 1 and 2

1. What do I worry will happen if I succeed at my commitments in quadrant 2? (This question is designed to uncover our fear and aversion.)

2. What am I holding on to that brings me a sense of security, validity or self-worth? (This is the attachment/clinging question.)

3. What am I believing/assuming to be true? (This is the 'Where am I deluded?' question.)

4. Is it true?

The first question, 'What do I worry will happen if I succeed at my commitment?', may seem strange on the surface, because everyone wants to live their values and commitments. However, our mind has countless ways to hide our fears from us and subconsciously hijack our commitments. Imagine yourself succeeding and then consider what negative things might happen if you do succeed. This question can uncover fears, so the body will often be triggered, generating strong emotions and protective narratives.

Let's go back to the traffic example. Imagine the stressed person's commitment is to be calm in traffic. I ask her, 'What do you worry will happen if you succeed at your commitment?'

Her body may contract. Strong emotions such as judgement and resentment may emerge. She might answer, 'It will mean that I don't care about being late, and that I agree with the stupid government who don't look after our roads!' (By the way, this is a real example from one of my programs.)

Next question: 'So what are you holding on to that brings you a sense of security, validity or self-worth?' This is harder to answer, and not necessarily needed.

In this case, she eventually figured out, 'Being angry on the roads gives me a sense of being a caring citizen, and caring about punctuality. It shows others that I care!' In other words, it was a very subtle form of image management. She was attached to being angry because she was afraid of being seen as a person who does not care.

Next question: 'What are you believing or assuming to be true?'

Her eventual answer: 'Two things: that getting angry somehow shows others that I care, and that traffic is the cause of my anger.'

It's usually at this stage people can laugh a little. When they state their assumptions out loud, they can sound a little unreasonable, and we usually don't even have to ask the final question, 'Is it true?'

This is the gift of shadow work: we usually expose assumptions that might have made sense to a five-year-old child, but in the light of an adult's compassionate, curious mind, they are seen to be untrue.

Let's explore this more with a leadership example. Suppose you commit to empowering people more. What do you worry will happen if you empower people? It may be, 'I'll become irrelevant as a leader because people won't need me.'

Move on to the second question: 'Therefore, what am I holding onto that brings me a sense of security, validity or self-worth?' With this question, we are uncovering our socialised mind attachments so we can graduate to a self-examining mind.

Your answers could include, 'I'm holding on to being comfortable', 'I'm holding on to security', 'I'm holding on to being right', 'I'm holding on to power and control' or 'I'm holding on to keeping the peace.'

This question is useful because all suffering has at its roots some sort of clinging or attachment, which is a fear-based response to life. And the more we let go of that attachment, the more open and slow brain–oriented we become.

The third question, 'Therefore, what am I believing or assuming to be true?', is critical. The human mind draws conclusions, then views all experiences as evidence of those conclusions. For example, if we develop the belief as a child that we're stupid, then throughout our lives we will constantly see reasons why this is true. This third question helps us to uncover all that limiting programming that we've accumulated over time.

We need to complete this question by asking ourselves, 'Is it really true?' If in doubt, we can ask people we trust if the assumptions we hold about ourselves resonate to them. More often than not, this will confirm that we need to revisit these long-held beliefs.

A strategy to loosen the grip of false assumptions or limiting beliefs is to understand how they have served us in the past. A common belief that comes up in Carl's coaching assignments is 'imposter syndrome' or feelings of inadequacy. The perceived benefits of holding on to this belief could include maintaining a sense of hypervigilance, seeking out additional training or deploying discretionary effort when things get challenging.

We then ask the question 'How is this assumption impacting you in the long term?'. Answers can include that it generates excessive stress, leaving us feeling exhausted, that we hold back for fear of being discovered as a fraud or incompetent: that we avoid opportunities for promotion or that we stay quiet in meetings. By taking time to cognitively identify the pros and cons of these hidden assumptions and limiting beliefs, we can exercise greater self-awareness and self-regulation on the preferred strategies moving forward, leveraging deliberate responses rather than unconscious reactions.

To make this process concrete, I'll walk you through the matrix using Mimi Huizinga, whom we met in chapter 3. Mimi is incredibly smart, talented and accomplished. Trained as a population health epidemiologist, she now serves as Senior Vice President and Head of US Oncology Medical at Novartis. Like most leaders I've met, however, Mimi's inside world can be a different story from what her credentials suggest.

She revealed to me, 'One of the most important factors in my growth process was understanding and admitting my core fear: that

I'm just a simple girl from Alabama who isn't worth much. I've always had this fear that if I didn't know everything, if I didn't have every single detail covered, then somebody would find out that I was just pretending to be smart and valuable and it would all come to an end. I have a high IQ, I have multiple degrees, I've always performed well on tests, I'm able to understand and articulate complex concepts. But none of that takes away that core fear.'

She told me how this fear has manifested in a few behaviours that limit her leadership (quadrant 3). She often wouldn't fully step up into her leadership role because she would think, *Who am I to create a vision for a team or company? Who am I to give feedback? Who am I to understand how this oncology drug works and to interact with the international experts around it?* In short, because of her insecurities, she wasn't fully giving her team what they needed: leadership, vision, feedback and coaching.

To change these behaviours, Mimi reconnected with her intent and core values in quadrant 1: intellectual curiosity, developing people and building teams. Her next task was to determine what specific behavioural practices she needed to better live these values in her leadership. She settled on 'Setting a vision for the team and then communicating each team member's value in contributing to that vision'.

'And how does this fit with your values?' I asked her.

'I want them to care about the team,' she responded. 'I want them to feel connected to the vision and know that their work has meaning.'

To help Mimi further, I inquired further into her quadrant 4 programming, using the same three questions. First, I asked her, 'What do you worry will happen if you succeed at your commitment to do better at setting a vision for your team?'

She answered, 'Then I won't have control. My team will do everything for themselves, and they will see that I'm not needed.'

'So what are you holding on to that brings you a sense of security, validity or self-worth?'

'Control,' she said.

'And underneath that need to control,' I asked, 'what are you believing or assuming to be true?'

Mimi struck gold when she answered, 'That I don't really deserve to be here.'

Was this indeed true?

With this new conscious awareness, Mimi was better able to understand her misguided behaviours in quadrant 3 and to improve her more conscious behaviour commitments in quadrant 2. She was also able to realise, and begin to own, that she definitely deserved to be there.

These kinds of insights help us develop the priceless self-acceptance we all seek. Possibly the greatest false assumption of all is that if we truly accept that we are worthy and good enough, we will become lazy, arrogant, selfish, irresponsible and uncaring. This could not be further from the truth. Indeed, the exact opposite applies: we become more engaged, caring, humble and open to growth.

Two more exploration questions on attachment

The attachment question 'What am I holding on to that brings me a sense of security, validity or self-worth?' can be the most difficult to answer. When going deeper with clients in a coaching context, we add two more questions to help us further explore attachments in quadrant 4. We ask our client to consider their quadrant 3 (unconscious behaviours) and ask, 'How have these behaviours served you in the past?'

Typically, people will react with resistance and say they haven't. After all, that's why we're doing growth work, right? But we continue to probe gently, explaining that these behaviours will have actually served them at some point. This question helps them shift from self-criticism to self-compassion to see where and how their unconscious behaviours developed for very good reasons. When clients can dig deeper into this next step, they often connect with some part of their childhood. Not only does their behaviour make sense from a childhood perspective, but now they can be more compassionate towards themselves. They see that behind their behaviour is an inner child who needs to be heard, not criticised yet more, and that resistance only supports the persistence of this behaviour.

The next follow-up question we ask is, 'How are these behaviours no longer serving you?'.

With gentle self-awareness, these questions reveal incongruencies in our behaviours, including the physical discomfort they create. This allows us to process our shadow, and slowly our attachments fade.

Completing the left side of the matrix

We finished chapter 5 by giving you examples of using the right side of the matrix. Now that you have a deeper understanding of the left side of the matrix, figures 9.3 and 9.4 (overleaf) present those examples again. For additional examples, go to mymatrix. themindfulleader.com and create a Mindful Leader Matrix for free or log in to your existing matrix.

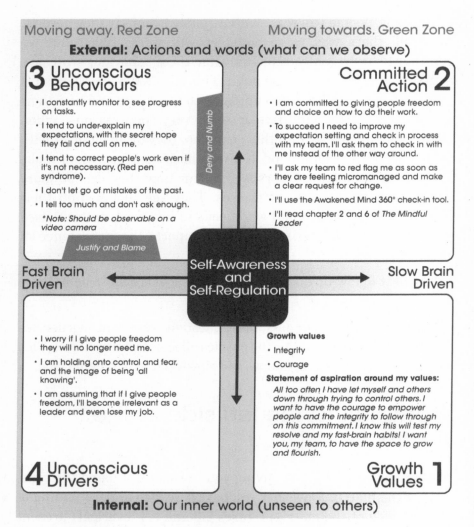

Moving away. Red Zone   Moving towards. Green Zone

External: Actions and words (what can we observe)

3 Unconscious Behaviours

- I constantly monitor to see progress on tasks.
- I tend to under-explain my expectations, with the secret hope they fail and call on me.
- I tend to correct people's work even if it's not neccessary. (Red pen syndrome).
- I don't let go of mistakes of the past.
- I tell too much and don't ask enough.
  Note: Should be observable on a video camera

Deny and Numb

Justify and Blame

Committed Action 2

- I am committed to giving people freedom and choice on how to do their work.
- To succeed I need to improve my expectation setting and check in process with my team. I'll ask them to check in with me instead of the other way around.
- I'll ask my team to red flag me as soon as they are feeling micromanaged and make a clear request for change.
- I'll use the Awakened Mind 360° check-in tool.
- I'll read chapter 2 and 6 of *The Mindful Leader*

Fast Brain Driven

Self-Awareness and Self-Regulation

Slow Brain Driven

- I worry if I give people freedom they will no longer need me.
- I am holding onto control and fear, and the image of being 'all knowing'.
- I am assuming that if I give people freedom, I'll become irrelevant as a leader and even lose my job.

Growth values
- Integrity
- Courage

Statement of aspiration around my values:
All too often I have let myself and others down through trying to control others. I want to have the courage to empower people and the integrity to follow through on this commitment. I know this will test my resolve and my fast-brain habits! I want you, my team, to have the space to grow and flourish.

4 Unconscious Drivers

Growth Values 1

Internal: Our inner world (unseen to others)

Figure 9.3: completed matrix example

Using the matrix in your personal life

Although this book focuses on vertical growth in an organisational context, the Mindful Leader Matrix can of course be applied to any area of your life in which you want to experience growth, whether it's strengthening your marriage, deepening your connection with your children, improving your personal health, or developing a passion or a hobby. You can take any aspect of your personal life and work through the first three quadrants of the matrix. Describe how you want it to be, which is another way of addressing your growth values (quadrant 1 of the matrix). Describe actions you can take to move towards your goal. Then answer the question, 'What's my part in this?' for quadrant 3 by describing the behaviours you've been engaging in that have caused difficulty. Lastly, explore your fears, attachments and assumptions in quadrant 4.

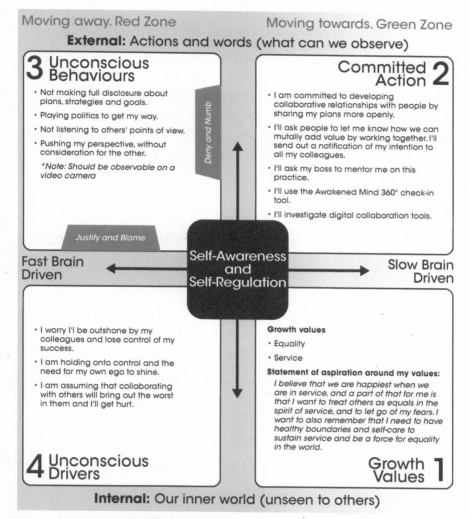

Figure 9.4: another completed example

Let's walk this through a couple of examples, starting with a person who wants to show up in their marriage more constructively. Suppose you're in a relationship where you love your spouse but you experience frequent conflict (quadrant 3). You want to experience greater peace and connection in your relationship (quadrant 1), so you identify the specific behaviours and support systems you need to move in that direction (quadrant 2) (see figure 9.5).

Question 1

Growth values: presence and compassion

Aspirational statement: 'I cultivate deep inner peace and quality connections. Despite a busy life, I find time to cultivate a place of inner calm to show up with presence, offering the best version of myself to my spouse. Through self-awareness, I self-regulate and make myself available to my loved ones by developing my listening skills and demonstrating patience and compassion.'

Question 2

Committed action (OBT):

- I meditate every morning for 20 minutes and take one minute every hour to reconnect with my breath.

- I listen to understand before voicing my needs, concerns and opinions.

- I use the Awakened Mind app to access teachings and audio to guide me and help develop my practice.

Question 3

What I tend to do instead:

- I get argumentative and continue debating my point until I win.

- I get frustrated and leave the room when I don't win.

- I go have a cigarette to take away the discomfort.

- I spend hours in silence and don't engage with my partner or the kids.

Question 4

Fears, attachments and assumptions:

- If I don't fight for what I believe to be true, people will step all over me.

- I am attached to being right all the time.

- I'm not worthy of love, and being right gives me value.

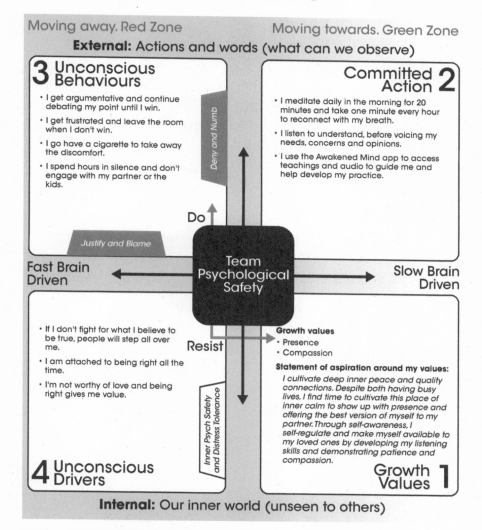

Figure 9.5: personal example #1

Let's use another example, this time on your physical health. Suppose you're starting to feel a bit overweight and sluggish because you've been working too hard and haven't been taking care of yourself (quadrant 3). You want to look and feel your best so you can perform at your fullest capacity (quadrant 1), so you determine what you need to change in your life to get into better shape (quadrant 2) (see figure 9.6).

Question 1

Growth values: discipline and self-care

Aspirational statement: 'My body is my vehicle for a healthy and meaningful life. Only with a healthy body can I aspire to a meaningful life in a sustainable way. A healthy body gives me access to the energy and clear mind that allow me to make wise choices and live a purposeful life.'

Question 2

Committed action (OBT):

- I program in my schedule three 1.5 hour blocks on Monday, Wednesday and Friday morning to go to the gym, and I walk to work on the other days.
- I go to bed at 10 pm after reading a book.
- I get Mark to join me at the gym and act as my accountability partner.

Question 3

What I tend to do instead:

- I take a few extra beers at night.
- I get lost in social media and fall asleep when I finish work.
- I sleep in and find excuses not to exercise.
- I say yes to all the work my boss and colleagues ask me to do.

Question 4

Fears, attachments and assumptions:

- I am worried about losing a sense of ease and choice in my life and becoming less happy.

- I am attached to numbing my pain through beer, social media and other distractions. It feels like I have choices and free time this way.

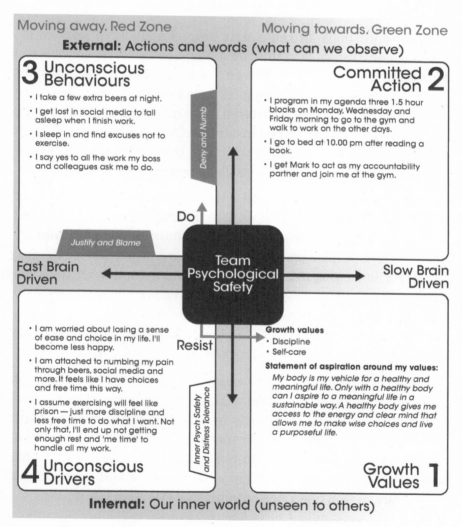

Figure 9.6: personal example #2

- I assume exercising will feel like a prison—just more discipline and less free time to do what I want. Not only that, but I'll end up not getting enough rest and 'me time' to handle all my work.

For additional examples, go to mymatrix.themindfulleader.com and create a Mindful Leader Matrix for free, or log in to your existing matrix.

Expect a messy process

As clear and simple as the matrix process sounds, in practice it's actually quite messy. Any time we attempt to overcome conditioned habits and responses, it feels like we're writing with our non-dominant hand or changing a golf swing. It feels awkward, fears arise, we bump against triggers and we often make mistakes. It's like learning anything new. If we expected instant perfection and no discomfort, we will give up. Not riding out the initial discomfort is probably the main reason we don't follow through on new commitments.

Expect a lot of difficulty and awkwardness, or even a feeling of immediate failure. For example, if you struggle with praising and voicing your appreciation of people, you could come off as fake initially and even lose people's trust. Sometimes it can take months for a new behaviour to feel natural and for you to and become what feels like 'yourself' again. Remember, your sense of self is really just familiarity with old patterns, so it's totally understandable and normal for you to not feel like yourself, or to feel like a fraud. Don't give in to distress, just embrace it and remind yourself it's just how the growth process goes.

The messy 'try, fail, learn' process of new behaviour practice will naturally activate the fast brain, and you will be tempted to alleviate the discomfort in the short term by reverting to the safety of past behaviours. This in turn will further release dopamine, a powerful neurotransmitter that plays an important role in the reward and motivation system, driving many of our reactive and unconscious behaviours. So you really need commitment through this process.

When we ask people, 'How's your practice going?', we're looking for this awkwardness. Are they making mistakes? Is it challenging? Uncomfortable? Are they learning about themselves, their fears and assumptions? If they report that the practice is easy, we suspect they're not actually leaning into it or their growth value, aspiration and OBT are not ambitious enough. If it came easy to them, they wouldn't need to be practising!

In addition to feeling awkward, most people also experience self-sabotage on the development journey. The journey can be incredibly demanding, even terrifying. It pushes us against our deepest fears and insecurities.

For example, let's go back to our micromanaging leader whose parents divorced when she as a child. When she began to really empower her team, suddenly the team that had been used to being micromanaged had a lot of autonomy and they didn't know what to do with it. Things were a bit chaotic initially, and she was confronted with the deep feelings that arose when she felt out of control.

The typical response to this scenario is for the leader to say, 'I knew this empowerment wouldn't work. I knew I'd have to manage my team more closely.' In other words, without perseverance, accountability and a growth mindset, it's really easy to fall back into old patterns while finding ways to justify it in our minds. In fact in many instances we are invested in conducting the new practice really badly so we can return to the illusory safety of our old habits and feel justified in doing so.

We recommend you be prepared for this. Expect failures, expect yourself to do the practice badly initially, but learn from the experience. When you experience failure, don't conclude that 'it just doesn't work'. Push through the awkwardness and the defeats by persevering with your practice, reminding yourself what you are moving towards and why it is so important to you. As Anna Fillipsen, at Novartis, told me, 'Changing behaviour is like building muscle. You can't go to the gym every once in a while and expect your body to change. Neither can you work on behavioural change sporadically and expect to change. You have to put in the work to strengthen those muscles.'

It helps to be kind to yourself in this process. Kevin Callanan, at Sanofi, offers a great example of this. When I asked him what he does when he realises he has violated his values, he said, 'I'm trying to be kinder with myself. So typically I will have a bit of a laugh and say, *You're doing it again!* I take a deep breath and ask myself, *Why are you reacting this way?* I explore the underlying reasons. I don't get mad at myself, because that's useless. I just see myself as a constant work in progress, and I'm okay with that.'

Map your vertical growth journey

1. If you want to do this online, visit mymatrix.themindfulleader .com and either create a Mindful Leader Matrix or log in to your existing account.

2. Think about the behaviours in your life that are habitual, give you short-term relief from discomfort, but move you away from your values and aspirations, as detailed in the 'Growth Values' quadrant of your matrix.

3. List those behaviours by filling out the 'Unconscious Behaviours' quadrant of your Mindful Leader Matrix.

4. Try to identify underlying fears or beliefs that could be causing the behaviours listed in the 'Unconscious Behaviours' quadrant of your matrix.

5. List those fears, attachments and assumptions by filling out the 'Unconscious Drivers' quadrant of your Mindful Leader Matrix.

PART III

Vertical growth in teams and organisations

10
Setting and living team and organisational values

'Coming together is a beginning. Keeping together is progress.
Working together is success.'

Henry Ford

On a personal level, the Mindful Leader Matrix helps you transform your values and aspirations into living, breathing, measurable forces in your life. On an organisational level, this is often referred to as *bringing the values from the wall to the floor*. In other words, the values on the office wall or company website are actually lived and taken seriously in the organisation.

Have you ever worked in an organisation that boasts a great sounding set of values—'integrity', 'inclusion', 'teamwork', 'curiosity', 'transparency', 'respect'—yet fails to make them meaningful through concrete action, leadership role modelling, rituals, rewards and accountability? It's not enough simply to state values and ideals. Organisational values must be backed by committed actions and behaviours, with real rewards and accountability.

A lack of concrete role modelling, rituals, rewards and accountability is the core reason why it's normal in most organisations to find the values on the floor being different from the values on the wall or website. This gap between what we experience and what we aspire to in our organisations can only be resolved through a values-aligned, vertical growth, psychologically safe culture. And this can only be achieved by leaders who are willing to do the vertical growth work needed to role model their own stated values in alignment with and fully conscious of the organisational values.

An organisation with a vertical growth mindset is one where everyone sees and accepts themselves as a work in progress. They are more concerned with personal and team growth than with protecting their image or status. They make a genuine daily effort to live and lead from a deeper sense of purpose, intent or set of values. This unleashes enormous amounts of energy, growth and trust in teams and organisations. It's not about who looks the best, it's about learning and growth. As Microsoft CEO Satya Nadella puts it, 'We need to move from a "know-it-all" attitude to a "learn-it all" attitude.'

Using the Mindful Leader Matrix within teams and organisations

As we have established, the process of the Mindful Leader Matrix is to free ourselves from the traps of unconscious fears, attachments and assumptions that create unconscious behaviours (on the left side of the matrix). We do this by consciously choosing growth values we aspire to, then identifying specific behaviours associated with those values (on the right side of the matrix, see figure 10.1).

At the centre of the matrix are self-awareness and self-regulation, which are the fuel that runs the engine of the matrix; without them, the process simply doesn't work.

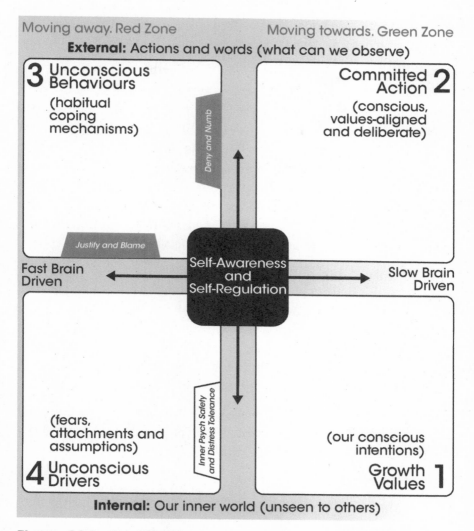

Figure 10.1: the Mindful Leader Matrix for personal use

Applying the matrix to teams or organisations requires us to follow the same general process. We see unconscious behaviours in our team that are creating distrust, conflict and a host of other problems. We understand that these behaviours are merely symptoms of deeper underlying factors: the unconscious fears, attachments and assumptions of quadrant 4. To overcome these issues, we first identify the organisational values we want to instil that will change our culture.

For most organisations, these are already set and, interestingly, are usually stated as growth values. The mistake most organisations make, however, is to use their values as an image management tool. This makes sense, given that the vast majority of senior organisational leaders are operating from socialised mind. Assuming this misunderstanding of the purpose of organisational values is realised, we then identify specific behaviours and strategies that help us align with the stated values more consistently and embark on a continuous growth journey around those values.

In an organisational or team context, there are a few changes to the matrix. First, we replace the 'Self-Awareness and Self-Regulation' in the middle of the personal matrix with 'Team Psychological Safety'. Just as self-awareness and self-regulation are the fuel of your personal growth process, team psychological safety is the fuel of team/organisational growth. In the following chapter, we discuss in detail how to create team and organisational psychological safety.

Next, we apply specific practical tools and systems to organisational change. When we help organisations with culture change, we use the 'three Rs' as the core levers for change:

1. role modelling of leadership

2. rituals

3. rewards and accountability.

Values-aligned role modelling of leadership with a vertical growth mindset is critical because nothing impacts culture more than the behaviour of leaders. So if we want to successfully apply the matrix within our teams and organisation, we as leaders must be modelling it ourselves. This is why we take so much time and effort to help leaders on their individual growth journey, as we covered in the first two parts of this book.

Rituals, which belong in quadrant 2 of the team matrix, help us to formalise and 'ceremonialise' the team or organisational values we're trying to instil in quadrant 1. They embed our values into the fabric of our organisation and make them living, breathing forces. Rituals can be reinforced by symbols, changes to the physical environment (for example, changing your office space to create a more egalitarian feel) and artifacts, such as pictures on the wall.

Finally, it's vital that we ensure our systems of rewards and accountability are rewarding the proper values-aligned behaviours. We're often frustrated by some of the behaviours of our people, yet those behaviours are unconsciously incentivised by our legacy rewards and accountability systems and practices. This is where an understanding of the left side of the matrix is critical, so we can see the unconscious assumptions in our systems that are supporting unconscious behaviours. Figure 10.2 (overleaf) shows the team/organisational values matrix.

With that brief overview, let's dive deeper into the process.

Using the matrix to set team or organisational values

When setting growth values at the organisational level, we use the same process through the matrix as we do personally. The first step is to 'make the unconscious conscious' by choosing what is important to us—in other words, choosing our growth values (figure 10.3, overleaf).

In the process of setting organisational growth values, we can't stress enough that less is more. When clients ask us to help them formulate organisational growth values, we insist that they choose no more than three core values.

If people cannot remember the values and what they mean in the midst of fast pathway–driven behaviours in the organisation, the values lose all meaning and purpose—they are inoperable. They stay out of the fabric of the culture, neatly tucked away on the website or gathering dust on the kitchen wall. This is why you need a 'less is more' approach here. We don't choose internal organisational values for branding or image management purposes; we choose them as a means to set an aspirational standard for the culture. For that standard to be a living practice in the team or organisation, it has to be instantly memorable and instantly applicable.

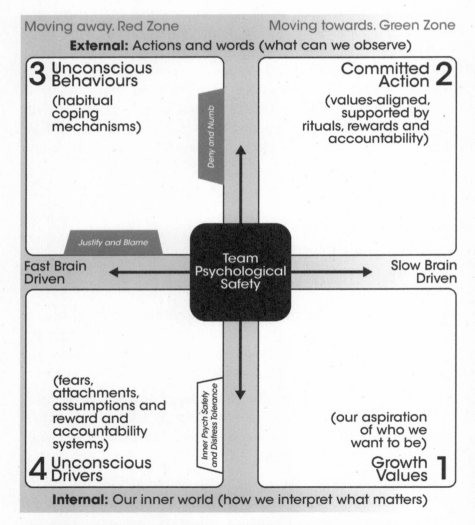

Figure 10.2: the team/organisational values matrix

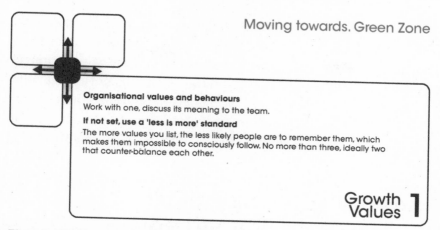

Figure 10.3: setting organisational growth values

When cultivating or embedding values for your team or organisation, our rule of thumb is to work collectively on only one value and one related behavioural commitment at a time. The team or organisation needs to develop a shared understanding of which value is most needed to move forward. This focus generates collective energy and accountability to begin the complex process of moving away from elements of the existing culture that no longer serve the team or organisation and towards a growth value (the cultural aspiration).

The behaviour commitment in the top right quadrant of the matrix is the seen action that brings the value from the bottom right quadrant into life in the organisation. Then, at a team level, use a check-in ritual on failure and success so the heavy lifting of accountability and appreciation in teams is done by the ritual. It can be difficult, and taxing on your awareness, to keep remembering your team commitments. A ritual is a constant, culturally embedded reminder of your commitments. At an organisational level, values-aligned behaviours can also be supported through rewards and accountability systems—we will talk more about these in this section.

As a tip, if you do have a choice to set your team or organisational values, the research tells us that the most important values for a team are honesty, accountability and respect. These values support psychological safety and team performance. The basis of a great team is people taking ownership for their behaviour and being honest and respectful with each other. That said, obviously you want to choose the values that are most relevant in your organisational context.

Translate your values into behavioural commitments

From the standpoint of organisational culture, values are statements of our highest cultural aspirations. They express the organisation we want to belong to. However, for organisational values to be truly meaningful, they must be translated into observable behavioural commitments.

For example, suppose your organisation lists 'integrity' as a core value. What does that mean in terms of actual behaviour? How do people behave when they are living with integrity? What is their behaviour when they are out of integrity? Unless a value is defined in terms of behaviour, it will remain an abstract concept and therefore have very little influence on the organisation. In the spirit of 'walking our talk' we share here our own organisational values expressed in behaviour commitments.

Growth value #1: Honesty

Honesty is the most admired quality in leaders globally and the single most important element of leadership growth, and leadership growth is what we do. To support our commitment to honesty, we keep these two key practices in mind:

1. We tell our clients the truth, no matter how risky or challenging. We are here to serve our clients, not to protect our insecurities or income.

2. We never gossip, triangulate or speak behind anyone's back. It's the direct conversation or bust.

Growth value #2: Kindness

We know that deeper development work requires psychological safety, and without kindness, psychological safety is impossible. We also know that kindness without honesty can create a lack of accountability and codependence, while honesty without kindness can be hurtful and even destructive. To support our commitment to kindness, we keep these two key practices in mind:

1. We speak and act from an intent to warmly include and befriend others.

2. We remember that no one needs fixing, they only need to remember they are already whole and worthy of the deepest respect. See them and treat them that way.

Growth value #3: Accountability

Accountability is central to all vertical growth. Without accountability we slide into blaming, denying and numbing; we begin to avoid what most needs to be addressed while becoming dishonest with ourselves and others. To support our commitment to accountability, we keep these two key practices in mind:

1. In any challenge or difficulty we first ask ourselves, 'What's my part in this?', and we own it and grow from it.

2. We hold each other to account for our agreed values and our commitments. We know accountability keeps us collectively on track with our values and aspirations.

Of course, we are not prescriptive in terms of the exact way our clients express their values. The key is that they are not abstract but are translated into relevant behaviours. Though we generally assume a common understanding of values, in reality people almost always have a different understanding of what is meant by values such as 'integrity', 'respect' or 'service'. The only way to ensure that everyone within an organisation knows what is meant by a stated value is to describe the behaviour it entails. If behaviours aren't clearly defined, we can't hold people accountable to them, nor can we reward or appreciate them when they bravely follow the values under pressure. We end up with a vague 'you're great to work with' kind of conversation; or, even worse, when values are not being followed we really struggle to have constructive, honest conversations about misaligned behaviours. Problems go unaddressed. This issue is rampant in teams and organisations.

One of our favourite lines of questioning for leaders is, 'What are the most important values-based behaviours in your team? Are they commonly agreed upon, and do you have rituals in place for appreciation and accountability around those behaviours?' (see figure 10.4). Most leaders we ask don't have these rituals in place. Our obvious next question is, 'So how do you deliberately cultivate a high-trust, values-aligned culture?'

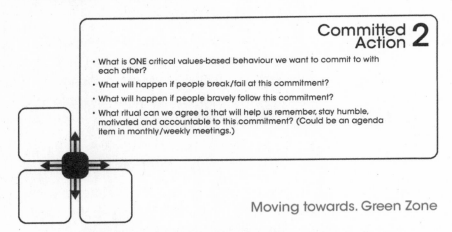

Figure 10.4: aligning behaviour with organisational values

To bring team or organisational values to life, it's critical to have a shared meaning and clarity around each stated value and its related behavioural standards. To give you an example of these guidelines in action, we once worked with an infrastructure engineering company that was building a very large civil project. We started by helping them to set their values. Although they set two core values, for this case study we'll focus on their value of integrity. Here is what they came up with for this value:

Value: Integrity

Behavioural standards:

- **We follow through on commitments.** This means that if we commit to a new behaviour, project deadline or anything else people inherently believe we have committed to, then we must take it extremely seriously and deliver—no excuses. If we know we won't be able to deliver, we need to have credible reasons and be proactive in communicating those reasons before any commitments are experienced as being broken.

- **We say it as it is.** This means we will not talk behind one another's back in this organisation, nor will we go home and complain about others at work if we have not had the discussion directly first. As leaders, we must make it safe for people to be honest; in fact, we must celebrate tough honesty so it is seen as a great thing to do in this organisation. We cannot leave meetings saying one thing and thinking something different. This will erode trust and ruin our culture. We need to say it as it is, and to consistently translate that into clear, observable facts and requests. We need to be constructive, not destructive in the way we say things, but above all we need to say it as it is.

So first they established the core value of integrity, next they looked at behavioural standards and stories. They chose two core behaviours: 'We follow through on commitments' and 'We say it as it is'. The story behind those statements is an acknowledgement of what it means and what leaders need to do to ensure it happens. It gives context, while remaining simple and clear.

Now they had clear behavioural standards to make their integrity value concrete and to hold each other accountable. Interestingly though, as we mentioned earlier, we encourage teams to simplify the process even more by choosing just one values-related behaviour in quadrant 2. Modern behavioural science demonstrates that the heavy lifting of growth is not done by a sheer volume of values and behaviours, but rather by the process of mastering of one important values-related behaviour.

One team we worked with decided they really wanted to focus on the 'we say it as it is' behaviour attached to the value of integrity. In the top right of the matrix, they could have used as their behaviour statement, 'We say it as it is'. However, they decided instead to use a subset of the behaviour descriptor to ensure it was even clearer and simpler: 'We never speak behind people's backs.' To instil this behaviour, they then looked at the three Rs of role modelling, rituals and rewards, and accountability.

First, they established a ritual around the behaviour commitment. They agreed to include a meeting agenda item every fortnight for team members to share one failure and one success around their collective commitment. They also discussed the consequences of people not following through on the commitment, as well as the rewards if they bravely did. On this front, they wrote down two things: 'When people fall into this habit, we will call them out and push them to have a direct conversation,' and 'When team members speak up bravely, we will thank them and make it safe by being non-defensive and curious.'

You can imagine how challenging it was for team members to admit failure openly when it occurred. But because this team had also looked at the left side of their matrix and had done enough self-awareness work around their own matrices, they were able to admit errors, take accountability and adjust their behaviour. And they were supported both by a collective commitment not to engage in shame and blame when people admitted to a lack of integrity, and also by a leader who was role modelling well. With this container of team psychological safety, they quickly began to appreciate and understand that the ritualised commitment would keep them accountable, help them personally to grow, and keep reconfirming trust and transparency.

In the simplicity of this ritual and the clarity of the singular commitment, the team's trust grew to levels none of them had ever experienced professionally before. It wasn't long before admitting a failure of integrity and bravely holding each other accountable became a team behavioural norm. In short, they became a psychologically safe team committed to a values-aligned, vertical growth mindset. What was particularly rewarding for us to hear was that their personal relationships outside of work were also positively impacted. This is one of the most wonderful parts of our work—while we help leaders, teams and organisations in a work/professional context, the learnings are equally applicable to other aspects of their lives.

Owning your organisational shadow

Shadows don't exist only in individuals. They also exist in every organisation. Your organisational shadow is what *really* drives your organisation beneath your nice-sounding mission statement (see figure 10.5, overleaf). For example, your mission statement may say that you exist to serve customers, yet your primary motivator is profit at all costs.

To look at this in terms of the matrix, the whole left side represents the shadow—our unconscious, unexamined, unspoken conditioning, assumptions, values and thoughts, which create unconscious, collective, destructive behaviour. Just as it does on a personal level, the organisational shadow sabotages our published values.

I once sat with the HR Director of a new client as she walked me through their organisational issues. In short, their eight organisational values were simply not impacting the organisational behaviour at all. No surprises there! But I was struck when she even teared up. It was clearly important to her.

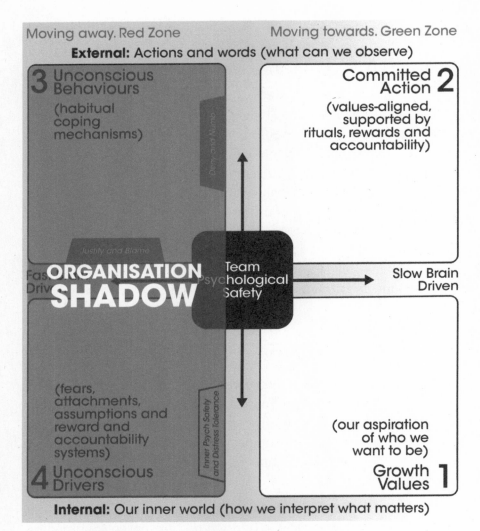

Figure 10.5: organisational shadow

I asked why it was so important to her to change the culture. She said, 'If you could sit in a meeting with me for one day and listen to the complaints I get about management behaviour, it would shock you. I can't bear seeing how much pain and fear this organisation is generating in people. It breaks my heart, and we have to do something about it.'

The incredible irony, of course, was that this organisation's mission was to help its customers with life-changing services, even while it was damaging its own people. Even more ironically, it prided itself on being a fun culture, with regular get-togethers and adventures.

This is the organisational shadow in action. There were a myriad issues. One of the organisational values was collaboration. Interestingly enough, the management team even had a large shared desk at which they all worked together. They had gone so far as to create this striking symbol of collaboration, and it was the story they were sticking to.

But behind their image management, the reality was utterly different. The level of distrust and outright dishonesty across the entire group was destroying innovation, morale and wellbeing, but it was hidden behind a veneer of smiles and collaboration. In some departments, we even saw a form of Stockholm syndrome: leaders who were clearly abusing their staff were getting exceptional 360° assessment scores when we evaluated their leadership.

As we've learned, the only way to stop shadow behaviour is to bring the shadow to light and deal with it. We can't be avoidant—we have to face issues directly. Until we can see the shadow objectively, we are subject to it. Seeing it clearly makes it object to us, which means we have the ability to choose a different path from where the shadow would lead.

When we began a leadership development journey, the executive team requested we start with middle management. Once again, the executive team was in complete denial of its shadow and viewed the cultural issues as a middle management problem. Fortunately, the HR Director, and eventually the CEO herself, got the issue, and soon enough we were working with the executive team.

Among many others, one issue we identified was competitive behaviour. Leaders would discuss things in meetings, challenges would be raised and solutions discussed. If a certain team member's ideas were not chosen as a solution, he or she would say intelligent but passive-aggressive things along the lines of, 'Okay, I fully support the team's decision and direction, but I just want to say for the record, that if it doesn't work, it will be because my idea wasn't chosen.'

I remember on one such occasion the CEO being simply stumped as to how to respond. She asked, 'Are you supporting this idea or not? What exactly are you saying?'

The person replied, 'Of course I'm supporting it. We're a unified team, aren't we?'

Passive-aggressive behaviour went beyond loaded comments in meetings. Dissenters would also subtly poison their direct reports against the departments whose idea had been chosen, then attempt to ensure failure. The aim, of course, would be a glorious image management triumph where another's failure would result in an 'I told you so' moment. (Of course it was a lot subtler than this, but the intent was the same.)

The hardest part of getting to the bottom of organisational shadow behaviours like this is developing the ability to get very clear on labelling behaviour objectively. In other words, if we are to name the quadrant 3 behaviours, we need to name them very accurately and objectively (more on this in chapter 14).

Slowly but surely we helped the HR Director and CEO precisely label the actions, statements and messages that were being used to create competitive dissonance in the organisation—the quadrant 3 behaviours. Here are a few key ones:

- When asked to attend voluntary collaboration meetings, x people have declined +85 per cent of the time.

- When asked to allocate people from their department to shared projects, x people have declined, using staff shortages as the reason, +90 per cent of the time.

- Collaborative projects whose ideas belong in a certain department end up being staffed at an average 75 per cent level by that department.

There were many others, but we will spare you the details. Once that was done, we also looked at the fears, attachments and assumptions held collectively by the group. The number one fear was being outshone by others and becoming invisible, thereby missing out on career opportunities. Just having that spoken out loud by members in the group was an important moment for shadow transformation (as the fear went from subject to object). The assumption included that only those who won at all costs would be successful in the long term. This resulted in all the attachment to winning, outshining, passive-aggressive behaviour.

We then looked at how the reward system might possibly be supporting bad behaviour. To our astonishment, we discovered that the bonus system in the organisation was literally like a golf tournament prize money pool. It did not matter how well you performed collectively as a group, nor did it matter what your actual results were in isolation from others'. All that mattered was your relative performance against your peers and how you individually were ranked. This determined your bonus. This is an example of a quadrant 4 embedded reward and accountability system working directly against the value of collaboration.

The resolution for this client's organisational shadow was multilayered and took us three years to complete. The work included:

- a dramatic simplification of the organisational values

- alignment of the reward and accountability systems

- a lot of individual vertical growth work at senior and mid-level leadership levels

- establishing new rituals for embedding the growth values in the organisation

- ensuring the principles outlined in this book were applied in order to build and sustain challenger safety (as is described in the next chapter on psychological safety).

Eventually, over the course of three years, staff turnover was halved, engagement increased from 'red flag' to 'best employer' level, and profitability dramatically increased in the midst of a challenging market. And there were no more tears of despair from our HR Director.

Map your vertical growth journey

1. If you want to do this online, visit mymatrix.themindfulleader .com and either create a Mindful Leader Matrix or log in to your existing account.

2. Take a first crack at creating a Mindful Leader Matrix for your team. What are your team growth values? Committed actions? Unconscious behaviours?

3. You'll want to keep on updating your matrix as you read through this section and/or advance in your development journey as an individual and as a team.

11

Creating a container of team psychological safety

'Few things help an individual more than to place responsibility upon him, and to let him know that you trust him.'

Booker T. Washington

Harvard organisational behavioural scientist Amy Edmondson first introduced the construct of 'team psychological safety', which she defined as a 'shared belief held by members of a team that the team is safe for interpersonal risk taking'. It's a shared assumption that others on the team will not embarrass, reject or punish you for speaking up or sharing honest mistakes, which requires an environment in which vulnerability is rewarded rather than punished.

Over the course of two years, Google performed a large-scale study to determine what makes teams effective. They found that the highest-performing teams have one thing in common: team psychological safety.

Team psychological safety is not to be confused with a lack of accountability. In fact, accountability for behaviour that damages psychological safety needs to be very strong, while performance accountability also needs to be strong.

In his book *The 4 Stages of Psychological Safety: Defining the Path to Inclusion and Innovation*, Timothy Clark identifies the four stages as follows:

1. **Inclusion safety.** Team members feel safe to be themselves and are accepted for who they are. In our *The Mindful Leader: Vertical Growth* program we work hard at helping each individual to safely reveal their authentic selves more fully to one another, from their deepest values to their inner struggles around those values. This propels a group rapidly towards inclusion safety.

2. **Learner safety.** Team members learn through asking questions. Team members may be able to experiment, make (and admit to) small mistakes, and ask for help. In our online course *The Mindful Leader: Vertical Growth* program, we take this to a more advanced level where we invite team members to experiment with their behaviour and admit to mistakes around their values and behaviours.

3. **Contributor safety.** Members feel safe to contribute their own ideas without fear of being shamed or ridiculed. In our experience, this stage is far more easily navigated once team members have already begun the values-based, self-awareness work in *The Mindful Leader: Vertical Growth* program. Ridiculing anyone for their ideas is a basic values violation. This is once again why values are so precious for the growth journey. They are themselves a container of safety.

4. **Challenger safety.** Members feel safe to challenge the status quo. In the context of vertical growth and values, they can also challenge one another's behaviour and actions in the

context of the team values and commitments. This includes the team leader. Challenger safety is the level of safety that is needed for an environment of vertical growth to be fully supported. Nothing short of this will do. Challenger safety is the most advanced form of psychological safety, because the very core of the ego and its image management defences in the team dissolve. This is the stage where innovation flourishes. We feel safe to challenge the status quo, or even the behaviours that are eroding challenger safety. We need constructive dissent, fearless dialogue. We cannot let rank get in the way of a merit-based discussion. As Timothy Clark explains, 'The social exchange in challenger safety is that you as the leader need to give me air cover in exchange for me giving you candour.' The intention of the challenge is informed by care and respect to support mutual growth and collective success. It's not attacking, belittling or demeaning.

Challenger safety is the essential container for accelerating team vertical growth in what Robert Kegan and Lisa Lahey refer to as a 'Deliberately Developmental Organisation'. It spells the end of image management and releases a massive amount of energy in a team or organisation because fear dissolves. As Clark puts it, 'A fear-stricken employee will give you their hands, some of their head, and none of their heart. And fear will eat your possibilities of innovation for breakfast, lunch and dinner.'

Consider these survey statistics from a 12-year Harvard study on the impact of low psychological safety:

- 48 per cent intentionally decreased their work effort.

- 47 per cent intentionally decreased the time spent at work.

- 38 per cent intentionally decreased the quality of their work.

- 78 per cent said that their commitment to the organisation declined.

- 25 per cent admitted to taking their frustration out on customers.[20]

Challenger safety delivers the promise of a truly values-aligned, vertical growth culture. Of course, without self-aware, values-aligned individuals on the team, the mission would be impossible, which is why we invest so much effort in the individual growth journey of team members. But even with evolved, mature people on the team, there is still a need for clear team guidelines that sustain group safety and awareness.

How team psychological safety impacts the left side of the matrix

Team values and committed action are not enough to transform culture. In addition to these, we need a deeper awareness of the collective behaviours and unconscious assumptions found on the left side of the matrix. Diving into the organisational or team shadow without getting hijacked by fear, denial, blame and justification becomes far easier when (at a minimum) the leaders in the organisation have done their own shadow work. It's even easier when the entire team have done their shadow work. The principle here is that the more psychological safety your team has, the easier it will be to work with your organisational shadow.

When we took one executive team through the matrix, in quadrant 1 of the matrix they came up with the values of honesty, interdependence and compassion, and the shared intention: 'We share our complementary viewpoints with candour and compassion for each other, accepting any related discomfort in the service of our success.'

To support these values and this intention, they created the following behavioural commitments in quadrant 2:

- Everyone actively participates in decision-making to best contribute to our shared purpose.

- We listen to others with openness, expressing discomfort as needed from a place of compassion and humility.

- We support decisions made by the team.

Once we had established their values and behavioural standards, we turned our attention to the left side of the matrix. We wanted to identify the unconscious forces within the team that were eroding their values and thwarting their efforts.

In quadrant 3, the team identified these unconscious behaviours:

- Members 'back channel' to get their opinions heard or preferences validated.

- We fall into indecisiveness or questioning existing decisions.

- We seek out excessive data when disagreeing or feeling vulnerable on a proposed direction.

What was the source of these behaviours? We dug deeper and came up with these unconscious fears, attachments and assumptions in quadrant 4 (see figure 11.1, overleaf):

- We fear being wrong, not having all the answers, the unknown, change and losing out.

- We are attached to image management as a way of maintaining credibility.

- We assume that risk needs to be maintained at very low levels.

- We assume that our individual teams are often more important than group solidarity.

- We are conditioned by the larger organisation's reward system of looking good at an individual level rather than as a collective.

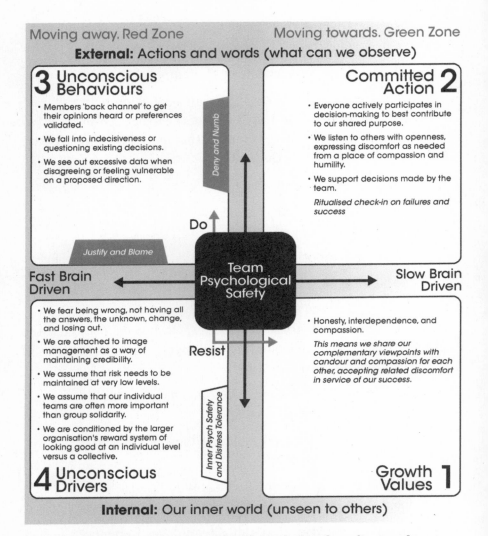

Figure 11.1: how the organisational shadow impacts values

Now we had a more complete picture of both the values and the behaviours they were trying to instil, as well as the forces getting in the way of their efforts. With this increased awareness of the left side of their matrix, they were better able to anticipate challenges and identify and address problems sooner.

But we still weren't done. We had identified the team shadow, but each team member was influencing that team shadow with his or her own personal shadow. We typically start with each team member's individual matrix. In this case, however, the team had done enough individual work that we felt comfortable starting at the team level. But after doing so, we then took the process even deeper and had each team member go through their own personal matrix. Here, we discovered some of the deeper personal behaviours and beliefs that were driving team culture.

Peter admitted that he moves away from his values when 'I seek out recognition and confirmation for the work I or my team does'. He identified that the behaviour came from his socialised mind attachment to 'being admired and valued' and his assumption that 'I need to know everything to succeed and be valued'.

Sherry shared how she violates her values by not asking questions. Beneath this behaviour, she uncovered the assumption, 'People will think I'm stupid if I don't ask the right question or have the wrong answer.' This revealed her socialised mind attachment to sometimes 'looking smart' over being authentic.

Andrew identified that he checks out and becomes quiet and impatient in meetings because he assumes, 'Getting lost in details is a waste of time.'

We could go on, but you can see how the matrix allows us to go deeper and explore the unconscious forces preventing us from fully living our values. But a key point is this: without a challenger level of team psychological safety, this shadow exploration within an organisation or team is impossible. Without challenger safety, team members do not experience the high levels of trust, respect and care needed to share their fears, struggles and mistakes, to be proven wrong in front of colleagues, and even more challenging, to call out values-misaligned behaviour or accept that being called out for their own misaligned behaviour is a moment of growth, not an attack.

Four key elements of psychological safety

Timothy Clark asserts that psychological safety is the product of two key elements: respect and permission.

Permission here means permission to participate in and influence the group (share new ideas, challenge ideas, even influence values alignment). Respect means inclusion, kindness and care, which aligns with Kouzes and Posner's research that maintains that respect is a fundamental value for leadership success.

As we climb this maturity model, the challenge is to strike the right balance between setting high standards on expected performance levels and creating the right conditions to ensure psychological safety is maintained throughout the journey. Figure 11.2 shows how Amy Edmondson illustrates this idea in her book *The Fearless Organization*.

The goal is to reach the sweet spot of a high-learning and high-performance team and organisation.

While we appreciate and fully agree with this general structure, more than 20 years of research on emotional systems and extensive work in this area has taught us that there are four key elements to building and sustaining a challenger level of psychological safety, and therefore a values-aligned, vertical growth environment within your team and organisation:

1. A self-aware, self-examined, values-based team leader is non-negotiable.

2. Triangulation must be eliminated, because it kills trust and disables vertical growth.

3. All team members must be fully accountable for their behaviour and agreements, and be enabled to hold others accountable. Defensiveness, blame and denial kill challenger safety.

4. Feedback needs to be totally honest, but handled with respect, empathy and care. Respect and honesty are non-negotiable values for challenger safety.

We covered the first point extensively in the first two parts of the book. We'll discuss the remaining three in detail in the following chapters.

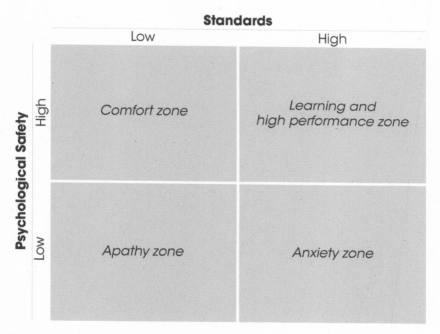

Figure 11.2: psychological safety and performance standards

Source: Amy C. Edmondson. 2018. *The Fearless Organization*. John Wiley & Sons Limited. Reproduced with permission of the Licensor through Copyright Clearance Center.

12
Eliminating team triangulation

'If you tell the truth, you don't have to remember anything'
Mark Twain

Triangulation is defined by psychiatrist Murray Bowen as 'a breakdown in communication between two or more people resulting in one or several of those people attempting to resolve/discuss the issues outside the confines of the parties to the communication'.

For example, suppose you and I are on a team together and we're not getting along. Instead of speaking directly to you, I complain about you to another team member in the secret hope that they might talk to you about your behaviour for me and resolve our conflict. This allows me to vent, feel better and shift the problem to someone else, while avoiding any direct conflict or recognition that I might be the one who needs to change my behaviour.

All too often the other team member will try to resolve my issue by speaking with you, but this inevitably backfires. In fact, triangulation creates *more* conflict, distrust and dysfunction. A consequence of triangulation is that a team's potential for vertical growth is squandered. People image manage and release their unresolved issues through sideways conversations, hoping to be rescued from challenging growth moments, instead of through conversations based on integrity and growth. And triangulation is not just confined to functional teams; it happens interdepartmentally and organisationally. It's rife in most organisations.

As long as triangulation is a norm in your organisation or team, your collective psychological safety, vertical growth and values-alignment efforts will fail. Like stepping on the accelerator while the handbrake is still on, your efforts will be wasted. To use another analogy, suppose you are trying to create a sealed vertical growth container where your team is safe to experiment, challenge and be honest. Trust is paramount for that safety. Integrity is paramount for trust. Triangulation undermines integrity; it drills holes in your 'sealed' growth container.

Not only that, but we know that pressure, if within a safe container, can be essential to growth. It can provide the 'why' for the process of development. Triangulation is a dysfunctional pressure release, which is why it arrests group growth. Leaders enabling or failing to address triangulation in themselves and their teams will find their growth and challenger level of psychological safety efforts increasingly frustrated.

The three roles of triangulation

Triangulation involves three parties: the perpetrator, the victim and the helper. For simplicity, let's call them Peter the Perpetrator, Violet the Victim and Harry the Helper. Peter the Perpetrator is doing something that Violet the Victim doesn't like, and she enlists Harry the Helper to deal with Peter. Harry closes the triangle by talking to Peter about the issues raised by Violet.

This can create all kinds of harmful dynamics that significantly impact psychological safety. One or both (usually both) of the victim and the perpetrator haven't developed the necessary distress tolerance, values commitment or self-regulating awareness to speak to each other from a vertical growth perspective, so the helper is brought in. But when Harry approaches Peter, Peter is upset at Harry, and now Peter feels like the victim. 'Why am I the one being blamed, Harry? You and Violet have been talking behind my back.'

Suddenly Harry the Helper has become Harry the Perpetrator. Now the original victim, Violet, is confronted by Peter, the original perpetrator (now the victim), and suddenly Violet the Victim becomes the helper. 'Well, I didn't say it like that to Harry, and I didn't mean that. I'm actually okay with how you behaved. I'm surprised Harry said that.' Violet is panicked because she still wants to image manage and avoid uncomfortable conflict and she says and does what is necessary to ensure things are smoothed over.

Of course, there are many nuances and variations to this process, from simple gossiping to entire departments or organisations lost in complex avoidances, politics and sideways conversations. Figure 12.1 illustrates the typical dynamic.

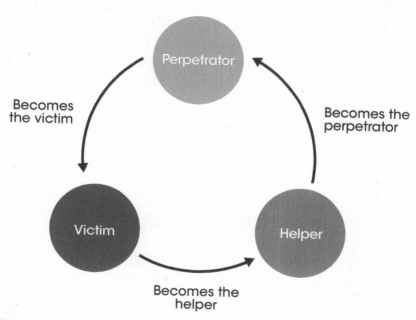

Figure 12.1: a typical triangulation scenario

Jenelle McMaster, at EY, shared a story with me about catching herself triangulating. One of the partners in her business was not performing to her standards. Jenelle suspected that she was struggling with a personal issue, but Jenelle was more focused on her performance. So Jenelle took her issues to another partner, and, in her words, 'We were amping each other up in this conviction that she wasn't performing.'

When Jenelle realised what she was doing, she took her issues to the struggling partner directly. 'We had two conversations,' Jenelle told me. 'The first conversation was me being honest with her that I didn't think she was a good fit for her role. The second conversation was more personal, digging deeper to understand what was going on with her, and asking what we could do to help her.'

This resulted in some really constructive choices and changes in the partner's role in the organisation. Everybody benefited. By stopping triangulation, Jenelle kept the relationship intact and was able to do what was best for the partner and the organisation. Furthermore, Jenelle discovered that her direct approach benefited her too. 'I reflected on my body afterwards,' she said, 'and I just felt so much better because I had come from a place of care, rather than internally fixating on her poor performance. I felt genuine, positive and lighter. It was a feeling of integrity for me.'

Over our many years of working with leaders and organisations, we've never encountered a team that wasn't experiencing some degree of triangulation. If you want a values-aligned, vertical growth, psychologically safe culture, this dynamic has to be addressed.

How to stop triangulation

The first and most obvious way to stop triangulation is not to engage with it when it's brought to you. For example, when someone comes to you and complains about another team member, or about someone in the broader organisation, you must stop it there and not take that complaint to the other person or to anyone else. You can empathise with the person who brought the complaint to you, and coach him or her to have a direct conversation. Here, you are directly supporting a vertical growth opportunity for the person.

If that fails, as a team leader your job is to offer mediation. You might say, 'Let's all sit down together and I'll make sure you guys really hear each other', while also both taking accountability for your behaviour.'

In these cases, leaders must be sensitive and attuned. Supporting team members to resolve their own issues is the ideal step, but it's not always the best step. On one of the teams we worked with, one team member, Jack, had an extraordinary ability to manipulate the truth and freeze out other team members from important projects. Tom, one of those team members being frozen out, had many direct conversations with Jack about his behaviour, and over and over was promised change, which never came.

Tom then escalated to his and Jack's boss. Their boss chose to advise Tom that given Tom and Jack were both in senior roles they should sort it out themselves, so he sent Tom back to deal with Jack directly. Nothing changed. Tom's boss did not triangulate, but he also failed to address Jack's flagrant values violations. He really should have taken the second option we suggested, which was to mediate a conversation between Tom and Jack. He also should have ensured they made some mindful agreements about next steps. And finally, he should have held them both accountable for those agreements. This would have supported Jack's growth and values alignment in the team, as well as increasing engagement and safety in the team.

The cost of triangulation

Triangulation effectively means the absence of direct, honest, respectful and non-defensive conversations. It supports image management, held together by fear and a lack of accountability, and is a hallmark of dysfunctional, psychologically unsafe relationships and teams. How many thousands of hours are wasted in your organisation on sideways conversations? How much broken trust is created? How inefficient does your organisation become due to insecurity or keeping secrets because you do not trust people?

But eliminating triangulation is not just about refusing to engage in it or holding others to account around it. It is also about providing the skills and environment where respectful honesty, non-defensive accountability, and conscious mindful agreements can be practised and nurtured. In this environment, people are progressively less inclined to want to triangulate, given that it's easier to have the direct, honest conversation in a way that serves team psychological safety, growth and trust instead of threatening safety and trust.

We'll look at some of those key elements in the next two chapters.

13

Keep the team on track with 200 per cent accountability

'99 per cent of all failures come from people who have a bad habit of making excuses.'

George Washington Carver

Several years ago, a major Australian bank was accused of having a toxic culture. The CEO declared in the media that the middle management was the cause of the poor culture. I still remember how perplexed I was when I read that. The CEO was publicly demonstrating image management and a lack of personal accountability — the very opposite of a growth-minded response.

Everyone is accountable for culture, but senior leadership is most accountable. Unfortunately, as soon as senior leaders fail to take accountability, they make it unsafe for everyone else to do the same. Image management becomes rife. Challenger safety is impossible. You can imagine how psychologically safe those middle managers felt about giving feedback to the CEO on his or any other senior management behaviour.

Unfortunately, this is not restricted to CEOs and senior management. It's commonplace at all levels of organisations. Over the past two decades we've guided thousands of leaders through live feedback sessions with their team, using our 360° assessment as the framework for discussion. Our experience is that, when leaders are confronted with blind spots and weak spots through their team's feedback, they immediately start defending, blaming, rationalising.

'I *do* communicate with you. You just don't listen.'

'I *have* to micromanage because I can't trust you to deliver!'

I will sometimes tease them a bit: 'So you're saying your behaviour is always justified and you have nothing to work on?'

They immediately backtrack, before often slipping back into rationalisation.

This is both common and understandable. We all have a hard time accepting tough feedback. We all want to be seen for our best qualities, and we want to defend, explain and justify our weaknesses. When avoiding accountability, we typically engage in one or more of these unconscious, fast-brain behaviours:

- rationalisation
- defensiveness
- denial
- blame/aggressiveness
- judgement
- isolation (running away), stonewalling, passive-aggressive retreat/withdrawal
- the PR spin (for example, we are told we are not delegating well, but rather than changing, we 'sell' ourselves by pointing out how excellent our results are)
- deflection
- competitiveness.

All of these fast-brain reactions diminish psychological safety. We've personally witnessed these on countless occasions while working with leaders and teams. On one occasion, the boss was doing his usual defensive routine. I stopped him and turned to the team and said, 'What is the impact of his defensiveness?'

They collectively answered along these lines: 'We feel unsafe and unwilling to give more honest feedback, even when he's asking for it. While he doesn't attack us, when he denies, excuses and defends, it makes an already challenging task of developing an honest team culture feel impossible.' They were affirming the absence of challenger safety as a direct result of his defensive behaviours.

On one level, it makes no logical sense to engage in these defensive behaviours. They prevent us from learning and growing, erode our credibility and diminish psychological safety. In fact, as I have personally witnessed, they can end careers and cost companies millions of dollars.

But on another level, these behaviours make perfect sense. We engage in them because they give us a temporary sense of security and emotional comfort from the vulnerable and uncomfortable feelings triggered by tough feedback. This is Fast-Brain 101. And as we've learned, fast-brain behaviours don't support vertical growth. Although slow-brain accountability may initially be painful or awkward, over the long term we are rewarded with vertical growth and the fulfilment of integrity.

Accountability starts with ourselves

A vertical growth mindset requires that we take personal accountability for own our behaviour and our impact on other people and situations. Without personal accountability, we remain locked in our self-defeating habits.

In his book *Good to Great*, Jim Collins presents a simple yet powerful analogy to explain how good leaders operate: '[They] look out the window to apportion credit to factors outside themselves when things go well (and if they cannot find a specific person or event to give credit to, they credit good luck). At the same time, they look in the mirror to apportion responsibility, never blaming bad luck when things go poorly.'

In contrast, when things go well, poor leaders look in the mirror and feel good about themselves. When things go bad, they look out the window to find others to blame.

We've done extensive research on how accountability impacts leadership effectiveness, and the results are astounding. We've found that 48.51 per cent of a leader's trust and credibility can be attributed to the principle of accountability (with a heavy emphasis on measuring how well they take accountability for their mistakes and misaligned behaviours). Furthermore, the difference in leadership effectiveness between leaders who do accountability well and leaders who are poor at accountability is 67.7 per cent.

Organisational scientist Peter Senge puts it like this: 'Personal change and organisational change are always two sides of the same coin, and the fantasy we often carry around that somehow my organisation will change without me changing is truly crazy. If we don't acknowledge this two-way street to change, we invariably buy into a "Messiah Myth" in organisations, where one person saves the day all by themselves, or we communicate that others need to change, but not ourselves. The first option ensures no one looks at themselves for change and the second option will absolutely guarantee resistance to change. Neither option produces real or lasting transformation.'

Unfortunately, leaders generally struggle with taking accountability. According to research by Graham Scrivener:

- 46 per cent of managers fail to take responsibility for their actions.
- only 50 per cent of employees report having seen their boss model accountable behaviour.
- 58 per cent of leaders do not keep their promises.

- only 35 per cent of managers share information so people can be clear on their responsibilities and understand company objectives.[21]

A simple question that helps you take personal accountability

If we're used to image management strategies such as denial, rationalising, excusing and covering up, how do we change and begin taking more accountability? In our work with clients we invite them to ask themselves one simple question to cut through all the layers of image management: 'What's my part in this?' This question, implemented at scale, supports the development of vertical growth, challenger-safe organisational cultures.

We deny accountability as a fast-brain reflex to protect ourselves from experiencing painful feelings, or distress. As we habitualise denial, defensiveness and blame as a life strategy for dealing with emotional pain, we increase our level of distress intolerance. The greater our distress intolerance, the more likely we will use denial and defensiveness as a means of coping with the distress, and the less possibility we have for growth. Simultaneously, we also make it very challenging for others to feel safe enough to take accountability for their actions in our company. And the lower the level of accountability, the lower the level of psychological safety and vertical growth as a team culture.

Sometimes in my work a client will say semi-accusingly, 'This growth work is uncomfortable!' And sometimes I get the sense they are expecting me to say, 'Oh, okay, then let's back off.' But instead I smile and say, 'Great! That means you're really doing the work.'

There is nothing wrong with being in emotional discomfort. In fact, you really need to expect emotional discomfort in the growth process. It comes with the territory and is a part of the challenge. Growth work is challenging, nothing short of a hero's journey. You are overcoming the primitive response of fight or flight, the conditioned response to run from unpleasant feelings. You are choosing to stay conscious and values-aligned in the face of emotional discomfort. You are making your emotional world object to you, not becoming subject to it. This is an evolution, a process of real growth.

Asking 'What's my part in this?' is a critical beginning to overcoming our disownership reflex. It's useful to know that when we ask it, our emotional discomfort will increase. Rather than worrying that something's wrong because we feel worse, we can lean into the discomfort and know that we're growing. 'What's my part in this?' shifts our focus away from what everyone else around us is doing wrong and onto our own behaviour. It marks the beginning of growth.

Tracy Furey, Head of Global Communications Oncology at Novartis, admitted to me how not being willing to ask this question created a lot of misery for her. 'Prior to Novartis, I spent three years at my former employer feeling bitter and blaming everyone else for not getting the recognition, trust and support I thought I deserved. I withdrew into myself and was really lost. I behaved passive-aggressively towards people, particularly my family. It took me that long to recognise how much of my unhappiness was my responsibility because of how I reacted to the situation.

'It was a terrible period of my life. And when I look back on it, I have so much regret because had I looked at myself and taken responsibility for bettering my situation, I could have gotten through it without the level of stress, anxiety and depression I went through. It didn't have to be that way.

'I held onto so many unresolved feelings. One time I was talking with a friend about it, and I had a moment of insight when I realised that everything coming out of my mouth was blaming others. I became disgusted with myself. That was the moment when I said, "It was you the whole time." I just owned it.

'Although that was difficult to face, it freed me to know it was my fault. It gave me the consciousness and power to look at my behaviour more objectively and to avoid my misguided behaviours in the future. Without that ownership, I never could have grown.'

Tracy's experience is common. Blaming others is an unconscious pain management process. We blame others to feel okay about ourselves, but ironically we are actually poisoning ourselves.

It's typical for leaders to lack the self-awareness to answer the accountability question for themselves. They tell us, 'I'm genuinely curious to see my part in this. But I just don't know what it is, so I'll ask my team members.'

These leaders often have a history of denial, blame and even punishment of those brave enough to give them critical feedback. This means there is no psychological safety, and team members have no incentive to be honest. So it's not unusual that when these leaders ask their team to hold them accountable and help them grow, their team responds with image-management platitudes. 'No really, you're doing great.'

This is why it's so important for leaders to work on their self-awareness and to the best of their ability develop the insight and clarity to at least partially arrive at their own answers to 'What's my part in this?' This enables them to come to their team with an already vulnerable insight by sharing and owning their shadow in front of the team. This does wonders for psychological safety and the possibilities for an honest team environment.

But don't expect instant results. If your team has mostly defensive, denial-based experiences with you, one single vulnerable experience is not going to be enough. You will need to be patient and keep doing the ownership work. It will change in time.

Two sides of accountability

When leaders begin seeing and owning their shadow and start demonstrating more personal accountability, it's common for them to recognise how they have been blaming others, but then to swing to the opposite end of the scale and take 100 per cent responsibility for everything that happens in their team or organisation. The truth is that neither the leader nor the team alone can be blamed for dysfunction and poor performance. In a challenger safety environment, everyone shares responsibility, and everyone must take full accountability — but only for what they control.

We use the term '200 per cent accountability', which means the leader takes 100 per cent accountability for his or her behaviour, and the members of the team take 100 per cent accountability for their behaviour. This principle enables the process of challenging each other in a team to become a growth-minded one, in which challenging each other becomes useful. Without 200 per cent accountability as a principle in teams, challenger safety simply devolves into no safety or scapegoating. It is that critical. Without the principle firmly in place, relationships and teams are simply unable to overcome really difficult setbacks or challenges and learn and grow from them together.

200 per cent accountability in action

I once worked with a CEO who was struggling to get his team to perform to his ambitious standards. He told me, 'My team members just don't get what it means to be a high performer. I tell them clearly what to do. I tell them this is important. They agree. And then they deliver substandard work. I told them I wanted to clone myself and replace them all with me. I need someone to help me teach these people to take real ownership and accountability.'

When I interviewed his team, I discovered several problems. First, the CEO's expectations were unclear and unrealistic. But team members did not feel psychologically safe to admit that, because they were already being accused of being incompetent.

Second, the CEO was micromanaging them while committing one of the cardinal sins of leadership and psychological safety: treating his team with disrespect by shaming and belittling them around their performance. Then the CEO undermined another of the psychological safety stages (contributor safety) by finishing their work for them, while becoming increasingly cold and distant.

Because they disliked their boss so much, they were just coasting, with no emotional connection to the company. Secretly, they couldn't wait to see their boss fail. Furthermore, if they could just tolerate a bit of noise and abusive language from him, he did the work for them anyway. It was a perfect storm of no accountability and no growth on either side.

I explained to the CEO that he needed to take some behavioural accountability. He needed to ask himself, 'What's my part in this?', because his behaviour was a significant part of the problem. It took some convincing and coaching, but he got there. When we met with the team, he acknowledged the negative impact of his behaviour and authentically apologised. We then focused on where he needed to grow and what needed to change in his behaviour. He needed to earn back the respect and trust of his people.

You can imagine how hard this was for him initially. He wanted them to change first. Eventually he agreed that he would ask for more input from his team, then set expectations using mindful agreements. He also agreed to differentiate what was truly important and what was not in his panic to motivate people. He had become trapped in quadrant 3 behaviours, insisting that everything was urgent and important.

To keep it tangible, in quadrant 2 he agreed to give people no more than three important tasks at a time. If something else became a priority, they discussed what needed to be dropped or made less important. His second big agreement was to leave people alone and let them do their work. This was scary for him because he wondered, *How will I ensure quality work gets done?* It created fear due to his quadrant 4 assumption that he was the only one who could ensure quality work and his quadrant 3 behaviours to micromanage to remove his fear.

That's when his team stepped up to take accountability. They said they would much rather be demoted, or get formal warnings if they missed critical deadlines or quality expectations, than be constantly micromanaged and shamed. He was blown away by that.

They made an agreement based on the concept of 200 per cent accountability. The CEO was 100 per cent accountable for changing his self-sabotaging behaviour. And each team member was 100 per cent accountable for delivering his or her outcomes. It was a contract of trust and accountability with clear consequences and accountability for change.

Five years later, his team's revenue and profit had nearly doubled and he was no longer engaging in self-sabotaging behaviour.

We learned four key lessons from this experience. First, to build and maintain a high-performing, psychologically safe team, leaders must take a vertical growth mindset towards team behavioural and performance challenges, and first ask themselves, 'What's my part in this?'

Second, accountability and growth are a two-way street. For the leader to safely challenge his team, he first needed to take accountability for his part in it and to change, but the team also needed to step up, take accountability and grow. Third, leaders must make mindful agreements to ensure that people truly understand what is expected of them. We can't assume that people know.

And fourth, if agreements are clear and respect is high, it's even possible to demote or fire people while still maintaining psychological safety in a team. In this case, when we did our first major progress check-in on how committed actions were going in the team, the team publicly agreed their boss followed through on his own committed actions while honouring the organisational value of respect. Once that first 100 per cent was established, he looked at the team members' performance, the 100 per cent.

One of them who had not performed well was demoted that very day, but with respect and skill. The CEO did not have to resort to shaming and shouting. And the entire team felt this was an excellent demonstration of accountability and values-based leadership.

Making mindful agreements

In our experience working with teams and organisations, we have found that most teams fall into one of two stages of development: *pseudo-community* or *chaos*. Neither is psychologically safe.

Here's how author M. Scott Peck describes 'pseudo-community': 'Don't do or say anything that might offend someone else; if someone else says something that offends, annoys, or irritates you, act as if nothing has happened and pretend you are not bothered in the least. The basic pretense of pseudo-community is the denial of individual differences.'

He describes the stage of 'chaos' stage like this: 'Underlying the attempts to change people is not so much the motive of unity, but instead it is to make everyone normal — and the motive is to win, as the members fight over whose norm might prevail.'

Unfortunately, we find that many teams cycle between these stages, from being nice but avoidant to getting frustrated and getting into 'winner-takes-all' arguments. Once these arguments subside, people tend to retreat back into the nice safe ground of pseudo-community. In the context of 200 per cent accountability, we get low accountability in pseudo-community, then cycle into destructive, 'I'm right, you're wrong', blame-based accountability in chaos.

Breaking the cycle can be helped by one simple thing: clear agreements between people. Note that 'agreements' are quite different from 'expectations' or 'demands'. People want to know what's expected of them. However, simply imposing mandates on team members is not nearly as effective as creating mutual agreements. Clear agreements eliminate confusion, friction and resentment.

Mindful agreements allow teams stuck in pseudo-community to create genuine performance accountability without alienating people. They also allow teams in chaos to hold team members to performance standards with more compassion and support. Instead of pushing or dominating, team members can simply point to the agreement.

Like feedback, mindful agreements are essential to quadrant 2, as they keep the team on track with the behaviours we're trying to instil.

Mindful agreements respect everyone's needs

Mindful agreements are conscious contracts between people that honour everyone's needs equally. They are the critical step to creating environments in which healthy accountability can flow.

One team from a large consultancy we were working with was experiencing real tension around performance and customer support levels. It all boiled down to a lack of clarity and agreement in the team on what good customer service actually looked like.

Some people made it a rule to always get back to customers within 24 hours of any email, even if only with a simple, 'We received your email and will get back to you' response. Others responded to clients only when they were able to resolve their request, which could take up to two weeks. The team members who responded in 24 hours got progressively angrier with their 'lazy' peers who 'didn't really care about the clients'. They pretended it was fine, but when a distressed client or two called them, they 'lost it' with the 'lazy' team members.

The reasoning of the 'lazy' members was that the '24-hour' group were 'over the top' and creating unnecessary, excessive work. Only when they all got together and asked, 'What do we agree great customer service looks like exactly?' that the tension was resolved. They decided a 48-hour minimum would be the standard for responding to all client requests, even if it was only a 'We're working on it' response.

They both eased the tension, and also created a simple accountability mechanism by which people could remind others to stay in the 48 hours or, if it was breached, to have a healthy but tough conversation around the importance of the standard.

It's a simple example, and of course some topics can be much tougher, for example on budget allocation or strategic changes. But the key here is that agreements are made and kept in teams. This reliably and consciously supports trust and psychological safety.

Mindful agreements are factual

We can't hold people accountable for agreements constructively if the agreement itself is not based on observable, measurable behaviour or facts.

For example, suppose a team made an agreement, 'We respect each other,' without defining what that means in the team. When team members try to hold people accountable to the standard, it can result in vague accusations, rather than factual observations, so we end up in destructive arguments or avoidance. This is exactly why we spend so much time with clients translating values into observable behaviours.

Since the standard itself is unclear, the feedback is also unclear. But it's easy to hold people accountable for observable, measurable behaviour. The policy of 'respect each other' can be made clear with a standard such as, 'We don't speak critically about others behind their back.'

Now when someone breaks the standard, leaders don't have to shame in vague terms; rather, they can point directly to the objective behaviour. The idea is not to blame or breach psychological safety, but to help bring the often-unconscious behaviours into self-awareness, while balancing compassion with honest feedback. 'Joe, we have a standard here that we respect each other. This means we don't criticise people behind their back. I have observed you speaking critically of Mary to others. Our policy helps us create a safe environment. Whenever you have a problem with Mary, please either take it straight to her, or bring it to me first so we can resolve it and not create discontentment in the team.'

Clarity on behavioural standards is essential for constructive agreements, as illustrated in the following examples:

Unmindful agreement: 'I need you to care about your job more.'

Mindful agreement: 'You have not completed your last two projects on time. We have a standard of personal excellence here. Among other things, this means we complete our projects by the agreed-upon time. Please make sure to complete your next project on time.'

Unmindful agreement: 'You need to work with team members better.'

Mindful agreement: 'We place a high priority on teamwork. One way to ensure this is through our weekly accountability meetings. I haven't seen you at the past two meetings. Please attend all team meetings.'

Constructive feedback creates psychological safety

The foundation of safety and trust is a values-based culture, and at the heart of that is honesty, which is what we want most from leaders. The challenge is that we fear that if we're honest, we will harm team psychological safety and create conflict and disharmony. On the other hand, if we don't tell the truth, we erode trust and our relationships become polite but superficial.

Accountability, honesty and respect must be integrated. The research backs this up. Environments with high respect and low accountability (that is, low honesty) experience poor engagement, frustration and distrust. Conversely, in environments with high accountability but low respect, engagement plummets.

In a study of almost 400 employees, researchers wanted to know how the quality of leadership during times of heightened accountability would affect employee outcomes. Participants were asked a series of questions about their level of accountability (for example, 'I am held very accountable at work' or 'The jobs of many people at work depend on my successes or failures'), job tension ('I work under a great deal of tension'), job satisfaction ('Most days I am enthusiastic about my work') and emotional exhaustion ('I feel used up at the end of each workday').

In terms of quality of leadership, the researchers were specifically interested in the level of abusive supervision ('My supervisor ridicules me' or 'My boss tells me my thoughts and feelings are stupid'). They believed that leaders who exhibited more abusive behaviours would experience very different outcomes from their employees in times of increased accountability than those who did not.

Of course, this is exactly what they found. When faced with increases in accountability, environments with abusive leaders experienced significant negative impacts on various outcomes, including job satisfaction, tension and burnout. In work environments where supervisors were not abusive, increased accountability actually led to better outcomes (for example, reduced tension and burnout, and higher levels of job satisfaction).

For a relationship, team or culture to flourish, they need high honesty and accountability, with high levels of care and respect too. Honesty is too often lost when we try to protect egos and be overly nice to each other. And we are often honest with each other in disrespectful ways that harm relationships.

Strong employee engagement is closely aligned with the ability to give honest feedback in a helpful way. Jack Zenger and Joseph Folkman undertook a study of 22 719 leaders to gauge how giving honest feedback in a helpful way impacts employee engagement. They found that those who ranked in the bottom 10 per cent in their ability to give honest feedback to direct reports received engagement scores from their subordinates that averaged 25 per cent. These employees detested their jobs, their commitment was low and they regularly thought about quitting. In contrast, those in the top 10 per cent for giving honest feedback had subordinates who ranked in the 77th percentile in engagement.

Let's now explore further how to give and receive honest feedback in a helpful way.

14

Giving and receiving conscious feedback

'Whatever words we utter should be chosen with care, for people will hear them and be influenced by them for good or ill.'
Buddha

My very first 360° assessment group feedback session with a leader and his team was a steep learning experience. Given that we always aim for challenger safety in our programs, we help our clients take anonymous ratings from a 360 report and turn them into real discussions. As we say to our clients, we are aiming for a culture where anonymous assessments of any kind become obsolete because it is always safe to raise issues without needing the safety of anonymity.

In these group feedback sessions, our job is to help maintain psychological safety in the room in various ways. But given this was my first time, some glaring gaps in our process were very quickly exposed, most particularly around how feedback is given.

I sat in the front of the room with the leader, with his team members in a semicircle around us. The data from his assessment was clear: he needed to improve in a few key areas. However, when team members gave him feedback in this live session, it came out in vague and accusatory terms. It was great that they felt courageous enough to speak up, but the actual content of their feedback—such as 'You need to be less controlling', 'You should stop micromanaging' and 'You need to trust us more'—was simply not helpful.

The leader predictably responded each time by rationalising and excusing his behaviour. We expected this and knew how to help with it. But what struck me was that the feedback itself gave him a general sense of what his faults were but was devoid of specifics. And as I came to learn later, it was critically devoid of fact-based suggestions.

We have a default reflex to defend ourselves, but it becomes doubly challenging when the feedback we are receiving is vague or accusatory. This session, along with a few other insight moments in my early career, led me to ask this life-changing question: 'If honesty is non-negotiable, if we treat it as a cornerstone of our lives and our growth, then how can we learn a better way to be honest?'

That question propelled me personally to seek out the best teachers in the world on the subject. It wasn't too long before I found myself sitting in front of the late Marshall Rosenberg, the creator of a beautiful body of work he called Nonviolent Communication. Marshall's work was not particularly well used or known in the corporate space, but its foundations were second to none. Over time we worked out how to repurpose his work for a corporate context. This changed everything, and very soon our feedback sessions became extraordinarily productive, precise and constructive.

Why giving feedback is so difficult

From a neuroscience perspective, humans have evolved to be liked and accepted by their tribe and community. Our dominant reactive brain (the limbic system or what we call the fast brain) generates well over 90 per cent (some say 99 per cent) of our thoughts and behaviours. When left to itself (unconscious, unaware, untrained), our fast brain is driven by short-term harm avoidance or pleasure-seeking patterns and behaviours. Each time it goes there, it activates the reward system and generates a dopamine rush and cortisol (among other things), thus reinforcing the behaviour for the next time.

When applied to the initial practice of honest conversations (when not yet a competency), the untrained mind sees potential short-term risk when engaging in honest conversations, as it brings about a risk of social rejection or isolation. Choosing honest conversations relies on another part of the brain, the prefrontal cortex and executive functions, what we call the slow brain. The slow brain cannot easily be accessed if the untrained fast brain is triggered. So an untrained mind, even when having chosen honest conversation as an intent or value (a slow-brain mechanism), is hijacked by the fast brain, which seeks out short-term harm avoidance and pleasure seeking.

With the right knowledge, practice and support and a psychologically safe environment, leaders can practise honest conversations, eventually developing this competency, with positive outcomes. The brain transcends the initial belief that honest conversations can lead to social isolation, as positive outcomes shape a new belief system through the reward and reinforcement system. In time, with awareness, practice and acceptance, the discomfort of the initial learning and growth phase morphs into new behaviours, as honest conversations are no longer seen as a risk or threat.

This is why training the mind through mindfulness and cognitive approaches (such as the Mindful Leader Matrix) is so important. It brings awareness and rewires our conditioned mind, which seeks only to protect us in the short term to the detriment of our longer-term intentions, values and desired outcomes.

How to give conscious, compassionate feedback

Obviously, to create a psychologically safe environment and vertical growth culture, how we give feedback is every bit as important as how we receive it. Here are a few principles for giving feedback in a way that helps people, rather than harming them.

Keep it factual

The first principle of constructive feedback is to keep it factual. Our fast-brain system makes assumptions about people's intent and leads us to confuse facts with judgements. We give vague and judgemental feedback, like 'You're a bad listener' or 'You're abrasive towards customers'. Neither of these examples is objectively factual; they are subjective opinions and character judgements, and more important they are not honest.

Please don't confuse opinions and judgements with honesty. Honesty is a commitment to speaking the truth about what is actually occurring or has occurred, not our interpretation and assumptions.

We also came to understand that when we speak judgementally, just beneath this way of thinking and speaking is an intent to shame or belittle someone. Our unconscious theory of change is that people will be inclined to change if they hate themselves enough or are scared enough. One can see why judgemental opinions in the name of honest feedback so quickly destroy psychological safety.

Understandably, the listener then gets defensive and reacts with excuses and stories. In contrast, constructive feedback uses observations that are free of judgements, labels, diagnoses, opinions, criticisms and evaluations.

Observable facts cut through defensiveness and drama. Instead of the accusation, 'You're a bad listener,' factual feedback sounds like, 'I told you the project was due today and you confirmed that with me, yet you haven't completed it yet.'

When we speak from blame and opinion, rather than facts, it is highly unlikely we will have productive conversations. When we work with clients, we have to dig through layers of evaluations and judgements to get to objective truth. We do this by asking a simple question. Suppose a client gives us this evaluation of a team member: 'He is selfish.' Our question in response is, 'What did you observe that led you to that conclusion?'

We then typically get more evaluation: 'All he cares about is himself.'

We press: 'Okay, what is it that he actually does that makes you believe this?' And we keep digging until we uncover the objective truth, the original observation. For example, 'When I asked him to help on a project, he said he didn't have time.' This is factual, not interpretive. Then and only then can we speak the real truth without judgement and begin a much more constructive conversation.

A colleague, Grant, was once leading a team debrief session where a team was giving feedback to a senior project manager. They were judging the leader as 'arrogant'. Grant asked, 'What do you observe in his behaviour that makes you believe he is arrogant?'

The team came up with a range of things. For example, he would often talk about his past successes. He had a habit of name-dropping senior people within the organisation that he worked with. Everyone on the team talked about the leader behind his back, but no one had ever confronted him directly. Once Grant was able to steer the conversation away from evaluations and towards observable facts, it became much more productive.

Observations have a quality of ordinariness to them. For example, the behaviours the team observed in this leader were really not that big a deal; they became exaggerated when team members attached evaluations to the observations.

As cognitive neuroscientists have found, figurative language, including exaggerations such as 'always' and 'never', activates our emotional brain much more than literal, factual, observational language. Figurative, or non-objective, language also delays information processing in our prefrontal cortex, as it takes more cognitive effort to understand. This means that using figurative language is much more likely to produce an emotional and irrational response.

Make clear requests

We're all used to asking for things. But making clear requests is harder than we realise. Marshall Rosenberg tells the story of a woman who told her husband she wanted him to spend less time at work. The husband agreed. Three weeks later, he told his wife that he had signed up for a golf tournament. What she really wanted was for him to spend one night a week with the children.

If we ourselves are not clear on what we want, how can we expect anyone else to understand what we want? For example, suppose you want fairness. You work hard and, in your opinion, your co-worker doesn't. Yet you both get the same raise. You bring it up with your manager and tell her you want more fairness. She values fairness as well, so she agrees. But what are the odds that you and she share the same criteria of 'fairness'? The concept is too vague for there to be much agreement on what it means.

Clear requests in a team context meet the following criteria.

1. They are specific

Clear requests avoid vague, abstract or ambiguous phrasing. They describe concrete actions that others can carry out in the present. The clearer we are on what we want from others, the more likely we are to have our needs met.

Vague: 'I need you to be a team player.'

Specific: 'Please make sure you complete your project by this Friday.'

2. They use positive action language

Clear requests are stated in terms of clear, positive, concrete action, rather than asking someone to refrain from doing something. Simply put, positive action language describes what we want the other person to do, rather than what we *don't* want him or her to do.

Negative: 'You need to stop bullying people.'

Positive: 'Please commit to not raising your voice to team members so we can feel more peace in the office.'

3. They are present

Clear requests are underlined in this moment. Even if what we want is a future action, what is actionable right now is agreement about that future action.

4. They are doable

Clear requests are doable. For example, it's not a request to ask, 'Show me you care about the team', because it's not doable. How would the person know what that means to you? A doable request might be reworded as, 'Please get to meetings on time.' If a request is doable, both parties know when it has been met.

5. They result in a conscious agreement

If we intend to hold a person accountable for our request, there must be a conscious agreement around the request. Without that agreement, accountability is a fool's game. After making a request, empathising with the other person's needs and coming to a mutually beneficial agreement, it's critical that we then repeat the agreement explicitly and create clear timelines and outcomes for which we can hold each other accountable.

All feedback should end with a clear request, otherwise it's simply a criticism. It's very common for us to sit in on meetings with executive teams. When the meetings finish, everyone seems to have an understanding of how to proceed. However, when I ask, 'Are each of you clear about the requests that have been made? Do you all know exactly what to do?', I'm routinely shocked when most of them don't.

'Makes clear and understandable requests when asking others to do things' is in fact a top five impactful leadership question among our 58 researched 360° mindful leadership assessment questions. This seemingly innocuous statement has a significant effect on engagement and leadership effectiveness.

My team and I have learned that this incredibly simple commitment to making all feedback a request is game changing. In fact, we have a habit in our work and lives of asking someone, 'What exactly are you requesting?' whenever we get vague feedback. It continues to amaze us how useful this is.

Check your intention along with your language

I've learned through painful experience that even with the skills we have just covered, whenever I have to deliver tough feedback, I need to first check in on myself to examine where my feedback is coming from and whether or not I can deliver it from a place of balance and kindness. I ask myself, *Is my heart clean in this interaction? What is my motivation behind wanting to give this feedback?* If we are mindful, our body will tell us the truth regarding these questions.

All too often I have delivered feedback that may have been true and necessary, but, because it came from a place of unspoken judgement or anger within me, ended up eroding trust. When I speak from that anger, I have no connection with the person to whom I'm giving feedback. In that space, that person perceives my feedback as a threat, not as something helpful, and they cannot be receptive to my feedback.

Alexis Serlin, Head of the Asia region at Novartis, shared with me how he makes sure his feedback is coming from the right place. He said, 'One of my mottos is "Complete commitment to compassion and decisiveness at the same time." Every time I give feedback or place limits on people, I first try to make sure I'm coming not from a place of anger, but rather from love. And then it's beautiful, because I can deliver feedback in a way that is loving yet firm, and it's received with much more openness. When we deliver feedback out of anger, the person we're giving it to wonders, "Are you doing this to help me, or is this really about you?"'

Paul Spittle, at Sanofi, added, 'Sometimes you have to do things that hurt people. But what I've realised is that great leaders are still able to be kind. Just because you have to give someone tough feedback, or make a decision that will negatively impact others, doesn't mean you can't be kind.'

The fascinating thing about this is that many leaders believe that showing care, compassion and empathy for others is a sign of weakness. BusinessSolver, an employee benefits administration firm, recently published the results of a study on the 'State of Workplace Empathy'. The study found:

- 68 per cent of CEOs say they fear they will be less respected if they show empathy in the workplace

- 70 per cent CEOs say it's hard for them to consistently demonstrate empathy in their working life; more than half of HR professionals agree

- 84 per cent of CEOs and 70 per cent of employees believe empathy drives better outcomes

- 50 per cent of CEOs and 72 per cent of employees believe empathy drives employee motivation.

- only 25 per cent of employees believe empathy in their organisation is sufficient.[22]

Don't forget appreciation with your constructive feedback

Although this chapter focuses on giving and receiving constructive, sometimes challenging feedback, we must also stress how important it is to use feedback to express ongoing appreciation of team members as well. I devoted an entire chapter to this in my previous book, *The Mindful Leader*. In this book, I leave it as a gentle reminder that your positive interactions must far outweigh your negative interactions.

Researchers Emily Heaphy and Marcial Losada examined the effectiveness of 60 strategic leadership teams at a large information processing company. 'Effectiveness' was measured against financial performance, customer satisfaction ratings and 360° feedback ratings of the team members.

They found that the factor that made the greatest difference between the most and least successful teams was the ratio of positive comments ('I agree with that' or 'That's a terrific idea') to negative comments ('I don't agree' or 'We shouldn't even consider doing that') that the participants made to one another. (We should point out that negative comments could include sarcastic or disparaging remarks.)

The average ratio for the highest-performing teams was 5.6 (that is, nearly six positive comments for every negative one). The medium-performance teams averaged 1.9 (almost twice as many positive comments as negative ones). But the average for the low-performing teams, at 0.36 to 1, was almost three negative comments for every positive one.

The goal of holding people accountable and giving them feedback is to limit poor behaviour and maximise healthy behaviour. In this process, expressing appreciation is vital. People who don't feel appreciated don't want to listen to us or change their behaviour—in fact, they resist our feedback. Finding ways to appreciate and recognise others builds trust and a strong team. By illustration, a Globoforce study reveals:

- 86 per cent of employees who were recognised in the last month say they trust their boss. This fell by almost half for employees who had never been recognised, only 48 per cent of whom say they trust their boss.

- 84 per cent say their company leaders are actively creating a human workplace. Conversely, of employees who have never been recognised, only 40 per cent say their leaders care about a human workplace.

- 86 per cent of employees say they feel happier and prouder at work as a result of being recognised, while 85 per cent say recognition made them feel more satisfied with their jobs.[23]

How to receive feedback with a growth mindset

The Leadership Practices Inventory 360° created by Jim Kouzes and Barry Posner is an assessment tool to measure leadership effectiveness. Team members are asked to rank their leaders on 30 behavioural statements. Of the 30, the worst scoring one of all is, 'Asks for feedback on how his or her actions affect others' performance.'

Receiving feedback can be one of the most difficult challenges for leaders, because it forces us to face our shadow, which is extremely uncomfortable. However, feedback is absolutely critical for a vertical growth culture. Feedback is how we ensure that quadrant 2 of the matrix works—that our organisation really is living our stated behaviours, and how we prevent unconscious quadrant 3 behaviours from becoming the norm. It's also how we do accountability well while maintaining psychological safety.

In a recent study of 51 896 leaders, leadership authors and researchers Jack Zenger and Joseph Folkman discovered that those who ranked in the bottom 10 per cent in asking for feedback were rated at the 15th percentile in overall leadership effectiveness. On the other hand, leaders who ranked in the top 10 per cent in asking for feedback were rated, on average, at the 86th percentile in effectiveness (figure 14.1, overleaf). Clearly, being open and willing to receive feedback from others is an essential skill for effective leaders.

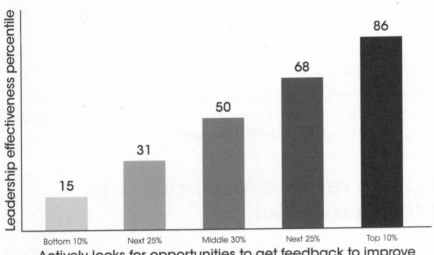

Figure 14.1: feedback and leadership effectiveness

Feedback is a check on fast-brain behaviours. It's an excellent mechanism to support and increase our self-awareness and self-regulation. If we can deal with feedback constructively, we can use it to halt our fast-brain responses and move to healthier slow-brain responses.

Selina Short, Managing Partner for the Oceania professional services organisation at EY in Australia, shared with me why getting honest feedback is critical to her leadership. 'As a leader, I do my best to constantly examine myself and try to be as objective as possible. But that's not enough. I also have to seek feedback from others. Because if I just stay within myself, I'll potentially fall prey to my own justifications or blind spots.

'When I first started my career, people were very hesitant to give constructive feedback. They wanted to be very gentle with me. But I urged them, "Just tell me. Don't put any good feedback with it, because I'll completely dismiss it. Be direct and be specific. I want to know."'

Defensiveness destroys trust and credibility

As I explain in my book *The Mindful Leader*, a feedback culture can only thrive if giving each other feedback results in constructive, growth-based conversations. It will die if it is punished and defended against in obvious or subtle ways. This is particularly true of feedback going up from team members to leaders. If that's defended or punished, a challenger level of psychological safety cannot survive. Not only that, but your values on the wall will always be different from your values on the floor.

We often ask leaders, 'When was the last time a team member gave you challenging feedback on your behaviour?'

Interestingly, many leaders respond, 'I haven't received any,' and they feel proud of themselves.

I respond, 'Well, that means there are one of two possibilities: either you've become perfect, or your team members don't feel safe enough to give you feedback. Which one do you think it is?'

Barry Keesan, Senior Vice President of Work Smart Learning, once told me, 'For me, it's actually a validation that I'm doing something right when my team gives me honest feedback. It means I have a good relationship with my team when they tell me when I did something that was out of line.'

When people give you tough feedback it's a sign of trust and of the highest level of psychological safety. When they withhold feedback, it means they don't trust you. And without that trust, you can't lead.

As we have pointed out several times, when we receive feedback, our immediate response is typically to go into defence mode. We deny, rationalise, justify, deflect, withdraw or even counterattack. When we are defensive, we destroy our trust, credibility and psychological safety with our team. Furthermore, we stop all growth and learning within ourselves.

Cultivate distress tolerance to receive feedback

Given that defensiveness arrests growth, disengages others and destroys relationships, why do we resort to it so instinctively? What's the payoff? The untrained mind immediately seeks to escape discomfort and slip into quadrant 3 by opting for pleasure or numbness—what we referred to in Part II as distress intolerance.

Taking ownership of our behaviour requires vulnerability, which can be extremely difficult to face. But, as we often say, 'Burning is learning.' Facing the burn of vulnerability is precisely what helps us learn, grow and create more connection in our relationships.

Cultivating distress tolerance through increased vulnerability is absolutely vital to a vertical growth culture. Without it, we fall into rationalising, excusing or counterattacking. With it, we can truly listen to and empathise with others. When people feel they can give us honest feedback, this creates more trust, and therefore more openness and connection.

Use curiosity to understand feedback

In chapter 13 we raised a question that helps us to be accountable: 'What's my part in this?' When we receive challenging feedback, there's a second valuable question to help us interrupt our fast-brain reactivity: 'Tell me more.'

We receive difficult feedback and feel the fizz and burn of the emotions that arise. We feel that desperate desire to defend ourselves and deny so we can feel better. In this space, we can take a breath, lean into the uncomfortable emotions and ask, 'Tell me more.' This is how we begin to cultivate curiosity in the midst of distressful emotions.

Then, as we sit and listen with curiosity, we can connect and empathise with the person giving us feedback. We can see how our behaviour is affecting him or her, and the underlying need behind the feedback. We can then create more connection.

Sometimes, however, feedback actually isn't constructive or valid at all, but simply projections and fabrications. In fact, that's one of the core reasons why people do defend themselves—because if they don't, then people can get away with unfair feedback. But using 'Tell me more' weeds out unfounded feedback.

If someone is truly being unfair, the worst thing we can do is defend against it, because now we give them the opportunity to say, 'I knew you would respond like this.' We give them that space by falling into the trap of defensiveness.

The best way to expose unfair feedback is to stay open and curious. It typically comes in the form of judgements and complaints, rather than objective criticism. For example, 'You don't care about your team members,' or 'You only think about yourself.' In this case, the next step is to ask them for observable examples.

For example, a team member accuses you of being a micromanager. Your first response is, 'Tell me more.' You sit and listen. If she continues with vague accusations, you ask, 'Can you give me specific examples of what my micromanaging looks like in terms of behaviour? What do I do that makes you think I'm micromanaging you? I'd really like to understand.'

If she can't provide a real example—something that actually happens—there's really nothing you can do about it, in which case the unfairness of the feedback is exposed.

Other questions you might ask in such a situation are, 'What exactly are you requesting? What specific behaviour would you like me to change?'

The more we can slow down our fast-brain reactions, the more psychologically safe, constructive and growth-based our relationships and culture will be. You may be surprised by what a difference such simple questions can make. After I had worked with one executive team the CEO came up to me and exclaimed, 'I had no idea how powerful these simple questions could be. People are really changing, and the *culture* is really changing.'

These questions become cultural soundbytes, which team members can refer to lightheartedly to depersonalise the awkwardness of working with new behaviours. This helps to ensure psychological safety throughout the process.

15

Personal transformation and the hero's journey

'You cannot dream yourself into a character; you must hammer and forge yourself one.'
Henry David Thoreau

The process of growth and transformation is a journey that can be scary, dark, lonely, intense and painful. It requires discipline and fortitude. It forces us to shed our false assumptions and habitual coping mechanisms to shift into a brave new way of thinking and behaving.

This growth journey can be compared to what mythologist Joseph Campbell called the 'hero's journey', which he proposed was the most common and archetypical story of humankind, shared across cultures and time. In a nutshell, he explained, 'A hero ventures forth from the world of common day into a region of supernatural wonder: fabulous forces are there encountered and a decisive victory is won: the hero comes back from this mysterious adventure with the power to bestow boons on his fellow man.'

Figure 15.1 (overleaf) illustrates the journey in simple terms.

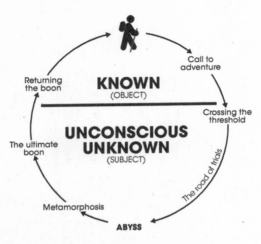

Figure 15.1: the hero's journey

All heroes venture from the known world into the unknown where others are afraid to venture. In adult development terms, the known world is all things that are object to us; the unknown world is all the unseen factors to which we are subject (the bottom left of the Mindful Leader Matrix).

The hero receives a call to adventure. If she accepts the call, she crosses the threshold from the known world into the unknown world. There, she experiences great trials. If she pushes through these trials, she hits the 'Abyss' — the deepest, darkest, loneliest point of her journey. If she can survive the Abyss and conquer her darkest demons, she is transformed. She is then prepared to take all the lessons she has learned on her journey back to her own people, who can benefit from her new knowledge.

The hero's journey in adult development

In adult development, the 'region of supernatural wonder' is our own mind. And mindfulness is the tool we use to navigate that region successfully. Steven Baert, former Chief People Officer and Executive

Committee Member of Novartis, shared with me another analogy of this process, 'It's like our mind is a 100-room castle. But over time we close all those doors because we're afraid of finding what's beyond them, and we occupy just a couple of rooms. Growth is about rediscovering the castle we live in and reopening all those doors.

'As we develop as children and we get hurt, we actually narrow down who we are as a person by shutting those doors to avoid pain. We limit our thinking and our possibilities. Growth is about rediscovering who we were before we closed those doors, liberating our mind and expanding our possibilities.'

To further explore the hero's journey and apply it to our own lives, let's use one of the most famous archetypal hero's journey stories, J. R. R. Tolkien's *The Lord of the Rings*.

The main hero, Frodo Baggins, receives the call to take the ring of power to Mount Doom and destroy it. He accepts the call and sets off on a journey, leaving behind all the comforts of his home in the Shire. He is immediately hunted by the terrifying Ringwraiths, but he pushes onward. The journey is long, tedious, and full of battles, reverses and trials.

Eventually Frodo reaches Mount Doom, which is his Abyss. There, he has to face his deepest fears and the worst about himself. Eventually, the ring is destroyed, and Frodo returns home to the shire, where he is able to use the lessons he has learned on his journey to help his fellow Hobbits.

In our world we receive 'calls to adventure' all the time. Sometimes they take the form of major life decisions, but more often they arise daily in the form of our emotional triggers. Every trigger we experience is evidence of something happening in our unknown world and an invitation to explore it. Sadly, we typically ignore or rebuff these calls, responding with aversion, numbing and delusion.

Accepting the call is the path of growth, but it also means facing our fear and pain. As soon as we enter the unknown realm of our mind we are assailed by all kinds of inner resistance. Our mind wants to stay in the comfortable, safe shire of our assumptions and habits. It's very tempting to retreat back into the shire, because the comfortable path is the path of stagnation, not the path of growth.

When we are brave we continue onward, guided by the north star of our values and our behavioural commitments: who we want to become. We experiment and fail over and over. We experience awkwardness, embarrassment, rejection. Sometimes it feels like we're moving backward, not forward. It's a very messy process.

At this stage we need a lot of support, accountability and feedback. As Frodo had Gandalf, Samwise, Aragorn and others, we too need wise guides, friends and supporters who can help us see clearly and keep us motivated. We must also cultivate self-compassion and patience.

Eventually we hit the Abyss. This is the place where we face our deepest fears and finally let go. Our old self must die in order for our new self to be born. Our socialised mind must retreat for our self-examining mind to supplant it. As Revathi Rammohan, at Novartis, told me, 'We all have an inflated self-image and we all like to think we are good. In reality, we are not as good as we think we are, and coming to terms with that can be really tough. Although the process can be painful, there is joy in learning and growing. But you don't get to that joy until you can shed your self-image and see the real truth about yourself.'

As we loosen the grip on our socialised mind and cultivate our self-examining mind, we find that some of the people and circumstances we once felt comfortable with no longer fit and serve us. In Frodo's case, he has evolved and discovers he is no longer comfortable in the safety of the Shire. In our case, if we make it far enough on our journey, we will find that we will move away from some friends and family members and gravitate towards those who share our values and priorities. When we do move on, we may find that some people in our lives try to draw us back into our old patterns in order to make us fit into their world.

In enduring our hardest trials, we learn lessons that can be learned in no other way. We have invaluable experience that few other people have. We can then use our experience and lessons to help others on their own journey. Figure 15.2 shows how vertical growth maps to the hero's journey.

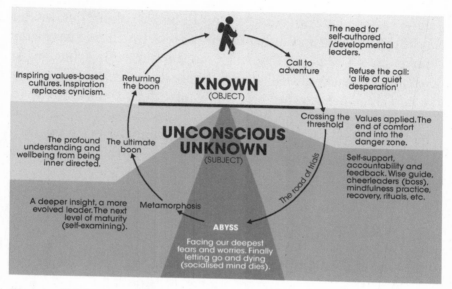

The need for self-authored /developmental leaders.

Call to adventure

Refuse the call: 'a life of quiet desperation'

Inspiring values-based cultures. Inspiration replaces cynicism.

Returning the boon

KNOWN
(OBJECT)

Crossing the threshold

Values applied. The end of comfort and into the danger zone.

The profound understanding and wellbeing from being inner directed.

The ultimate boon

UNCONSCIOUS UNKNOWN
(SUBJECT)

The road of trials

Self-support, accountability and feedback. Wise guide, cheerleaders (boss), mindfulness practice, recovery, rituals, etc.

A deeper insight, a more evolved leader. The next level of maturity (self-examining).

Metamorphosis

ABYSS

Facing our deepest fears and worries. Finally letting go and dying (socialised mind dies).

Figure 15.2: vertical growth on the hero's journey

Be kind to yourself on the journey

Growth can be excruciating. It forces us to confront the most painful truths about ourselves, to recognise our patterns of behaviour that harm others and limit ourselves. If we add harsh judgement and self-criticism to that process, it frequently becomes too painful for us to grow. We shut down the process because we're not giving ourselves enough kindness and compassion.

I asked Anna Fillipsen, at Novartis, to share with me the best advice she would give to anyone embarking on a growth journey. She said, 'To stay in this process you have to really learn how to take care of yourself. Take care of your heart so you can open up and be vulnerable with yourself and the issues you're facing. Support yourself so you can become stronger in the process, instead of being beaten up by it.

'In the past I've beaten myself up much more and for much longer than I should have. If I could do it over again, I would be much kinder and more compassionate with myself. It's the only way to be vulnerable with my fears and limitations in the most authentic way.'

If we can be kind with ourselves, Alexis Serlin pointed out, we can also be more honest and authentic with others, which creates greater connection. As he put it, 'Looking great and protecting your image does not connect you with people. People don't like robots — they like human beings who are beautifully imperfect. You don't have to have all the answers. You don't have to be in control. You can show your flaws and your insecurities. You can accept the fact that you are beautifully imperfect, and you can still enjoy the journey and have an impact on others.'

Be true to yourself

Ultimately, the hero's journey is less about our developing into something than about coming home to who we already are, underneath all our self-doubt and self-criticism, underneath our mentally constructed identity. It's about giving up our attachment to patterns that no longer serve us, letting them die along with the constructed identity we built through those patterns.

The spiritual teacher Eckhart Tolle observed, 'Death is a stripping away of all that is not you. The secret of life is to "die before you die" — and find that there is no death.' Mastering ourselves is more about removal than addition. It's about stripping off the masks and images that we use to impress people, but that keep us feeling isolated. It's about letting go of beliefs and ideas that keep us locked in self-defeating habits. It's about dissolving the inner judge, surrendering the burden of a busy mind, and rediscovering the innate love and wisdom that have been with us all along.

As we let go, we begin to connect with our deepest, truest selves. In a sense, we take Pinocchio's journey. Through a commitment to honesty, we become real and authentic, and our artificial selves fade away. As the parts of us that we want to hide from ourselves and the world are revealed, we are empowered to fully embrace our whole selves. This is how we find authentic joy and meaning in our lives.

In this process, we evolve from socialised mind to self-examining mind to awakened mind. In self-examining mind, we can consciously choose our values and what we want our lives to be about, rather than catering to how everyone else wants us to live. In this state, not only can we lead our own lives better, but we also become better leaders to others.

Susanne Schaffert, at Novartis, told me, 'As a leader, you have tons of demands placed on you. You have to be clear with yourself, know your values and boundaries, and stay true to them. If you're in a company that tells you to change your beliefs, values and style, you're in the wrong place. You have to be yourself. When I'm 80 years old and looking back on my life, I want to remember that I was always true to my values. I was always honest, I always cared about the people around me.'

Living and leading from wholesome values is truly the 'hero's journey', the metamorphosis of the caterpillar into the butterfly. Our fundamental source of wellbeing has shifted from the fluid and unpredictable external world to an inner compass of wholesome values. The journey challenges us to the very core. But we take it courageously to gain the wisdom and peace that can come only from living in alignment with our core, life-serving values.

May you be well, my friend.

The Mindful Leader: Vertical Growth Resources

The Mindful Leader: Vertical Growth Online Course

themindfulleader.com/Vertical-Growth-Online-Course

If you would like additional guidance, our evidenced-based, structured development online course is designed to support you to become sustainably growth based even long after the program is complete.

The Mindful Leader: Vertical Growth Program for Teams and Organisations

themindfulleader.com

If your team or organisation wants to develop a values-aligned, growth-based, psychologically safe culture, visit our website to learn more about our Keynote Series, Leadership Assessment & Leadership Program.

Sources

1. Harter, J. (2022). U.S. employee engagement drops for first year in a decade. Gallup, January 7.

2. Colier, N. (2019). Negative thinking: a dangerous addiction. *Psychology today.*

3. Yeats, D. A. (n.d.). A summary of Susanne Cook-Greuter's developmental model. davidayeats.com

4. Park, N., Peterson, C., & Seligman, M. E. (2004). Strengths of character and well-being. *Journal of Social and Clinical Psychology, 23*(5), 603–19.

5. Hudson-Searle, G. (2020). *Purposeful Discussions.* Troubador Publishing Limited.

6. Kasala, E. R., Bodduluru, L. N., Maneti, Y., & Thipparaboina, R. (2014). Effect of meditation on neurophysiological changes in stress mediated depression. *Complementary therapies in clinical practice, 20*(1), 74–80. Jung, Y. H., Kang, D. H., Jang, J. H., Park, H. Y., et al. (2010). The effects of mind–body training on stress reduction, positive affect, and plasma catecholamines. *Neuroscience letters, 479*(2), 138–42.

7. Newberg, A. B., & Iversen, J. (2003). The neural basis of the complex mental task of meditation: neurotransmitter and neurochemical considerations. *Medical hypotheses, 61*(2), 282–91. Kasala, E. R., Bodduluru, L. N., Maneti, Y., & Thipparaboina, R.

(2014). Effect of meditation on neurophysiological changes in stress mediated depression. *Complementary therapies in clinical practice*, *20*(1), 74–80.

8. Davidson, R. J., Kabat-Zinn, J., Schumacher, J., Rosenkranz, M., et al. (2003). Alterations in brain and immune function produced by mindfulness meditation. *Psychosomatic medicine*, *65*(4), 564–70. Kasala, E. R., Bodduluru, L. N., Maneti, Y., & Thipparaboina, R. (2014). Effect of meditation on neurophysiological changes in stress mediated depression. *Complementary therapies in clinical practice*, *20*(1), 74–80.

9. Tang, Y. Y., Hölzel, B. K., & Posner, M. I. (2015). The neuroscience of mindfulness meditation. *Nature Reviews Neuroscience*, *16*(4), 213–25. Fox, K. C., Nijeboer, S., Dixon, M. L., Floman, J. L., et al. (2014). Is meditation associated with altered brain structure? A systematic review and meta-analysis of morphometric neuroimaging in meditation practitioners. *Neuroscience & Biobehavioural Reviews*, *43*, 48–73.

10. Lazar, S. W., Kerr, C. E., Wasserman, R. H., Gray, et al. (2005). Meditation experience is associated with increased cortical thickness. *Neuroreport*, *16*(17), 1893.

11. Tang, Y. Y., Lu, Q., Geng, X., Stein, E. A., et al. (2010). Short-term meditation induces white matter changes in the anterior cingulate. *Proceedings of the National Academy of Sciences*, *107*(35), 15649–52.

12. Tang, Y. Y., Hölzel, B. K., & Posner, M. I. (2015). The neuroscience of mindfulness meditation. *Nature Reviews Neuroscience*, *16*(4), 213–25.

13. Tang, Y. Y., Rothbart, M. K., & Posner, M. I. (2012). Neural correlates of establishing, maintaining, and switching brain states. *Trends in cognitive sciences*, *16*(6), 330–37.

14. Tang, Y. Y., Ma, Y., Wang, J., Fan, Y., et al. (2007). Short-term meditation training improves attention and self-regulation. *Proceedings of the National Academy of Sciences*, *104*(43),

17152–56. Tang, Y. Y., Hölzel, B. K., & Posner, M. I. (2015). The neuroscience of mindfulness meditation. *Nature Reviews Neuroscience*, *16*(4), 213–25.

15. David, S. (2018). The gift and power of emotional courage, TED talk.

16. Government of Western Australia, Centre for Clinical Interventions, Tolerating distress, Resources, https://www.cci .health.wa.gov.au/

17. Carpenter, J. K., Sanford, J., & Hofmann, S. G. (2019). The effect of brief mindfulness training on distress tolerance and stress reactivity. *Behavior therapy*, *50*(3), 630–45.

18. In JoAnne Dahl et al. (2009). *The Art and Science of Valuing in Psychotherapy*. New Harbinger Publications.

19. David, S. (2018). The gift and power of emotional courage, TED talk.

20. Porath, C., & Pearson, C. (2013). The price of incivility. *Harvard Business Review*, January–February.

21. Scrivener, G. (2015). Why being accountable matters. trainingzone.co.uk, January 12.

22. Businessolver® 2021 State of Workplace Empathy Executive Summary, Businessolver.com; all rights reserved.

23. Mosley, E. (2016). 4 reasons employee appreciation matters year-round. *HuffPost*, the blog. March 3.

Index